Web Performance Daybook, Volume 2

Edited by Stoyan Stefanov

O'REILLY®

Beijing · Cambridge · Farnham · Köln · Sebastopol · Tokyo

Web Performance Daybook, Volume 2

Edited by Stoyan Stefanov

Published by O'Reilly Media, Inc., 1005 Gravenstein Highway North, Sebastopol, CA 95472.

O'Reilly books may be purchased for educational, business, or sales promotional use. Online editions are also available for most titles (*http://my.safaribooksonline.com*). For more information, contact our corporate/institutional sales department: 800-998-9938 or *corporate@oreilly.com*.

Editor: Mary Treseler
Production Editor: Melanie Yarbrough
Proofreader: Nancy Reinhardt

Cover Designer: Karen Montgomery
Interior Designer: David Futato
Illustrator: Robert Romano

June 2012:   First Edition.

Revision History for the First Edition:
     2012-06-15   First release
See *http://oreilly.com/catalog/errata.csp?isbn=9781449332914* for release details.

ISBN: 978-1-449-33291-4

[LSI]

1339598811

Table of Contents

Foreword

In your hands is the largest collection of web performance articles ever published. It includes performance topics such as open source tools, caching, mobile networks and applications, automation, improving the user experience, HTML5, JavaScript, CSS3, metrics, ROI, and network protocols. The collection of authors is diverse including employees of the world's largest web companies to independent consultants. At least seven web performance startups are represented among the contributors: Blaze, Cloud-Flare, Log Normal, Strangeloop, Torbit, Turbobytes, and Zoompf. The range of topics and contributors is impressive. But what really impresses me is that, in addition to their day jobs, every contributor also runs one or more open source projects, blogs, writes books, speaks at conferences, organizes meetups, or runs a non-profit. Some do all of these. After a full day of taming JavaScript across a dozen major browsers or tracking down the regression that made page load times spike, what compels these people to contribute back to the web performance community during their "spare time"? Here are some of the responses I've received when asking this question:

Lack of Formal Training

Many of us working on the Web learned our craft on the job. Web stuff either wasn't in our college curriculum or what we did learn isn't applicable to what we do now. This on the job training is a long process involving a lot of trial and error. Sharing best practices raises the group IQ and lets new people entering the field come up to speed more quickly.

Avoid Repeating the Same Mistakes

Mistakes happen during this trial and error process. Sometimes a lot of mistakes happen. We have all experienced banging our heads against a problem in the wee hours of the morning or for days on end, often stumbling on the solution only after a long process of elimination. Thankfully, our sense of community doesn't allow us to stand by mutely while we watch our peers heading for the same pitfalls. Sharing the solutions we found lets others avoid the same mistakes we made.

Obsessed with Optimization

By their nature, developers are drawn to optimization. We all strive to make our code the fastest, our algorithms the most efficient, and our architectures the most resilient. This obsession doesn't just stop with our website; we want every website to be optimized. The best way to do that is to share what we know.

Like to Help

Finally, some people just really like to help others. That look on someone's face when they realize they just saved a week of work or made their site twice as fast makes us feel like we've helped the community grow.

As a testimony to this sense of sharing, the authors have dedicated all royalties of this book to the WPO Foundation, a non-profit organization that supports the web performance community. Thus, you can enjoy the chapters that lie ahead not only because they are some of the best web performance advice on the planet, but also because it was given to the web performance community selflessly. Enjoy!

—Steve Souders

From the Editor

In the spirit of the true high-performance, non-blocking asynchronous delivery, you now have the *Web Performance Daybook, Volume 2* published before Volume 1. I hope you'll enjoy reading the book as much as I enjoyed working on it and rubbing (virtual) shoulders with some of the brightest people in our industry.

Back in December 2009, I wanted to give an overview of the web performance optimization (WPO) discipline. I decided on a self-imposed deadline of an-article-a-day from December 1 to 24: the format of an advent calendar similar to *http://www.24ways .org*. As it turned out, 24 articles in a row was quite a challenge and so I was happy and grateful to accept the offers for help from a few friends from the industry: Christian Heilmann (Mozilla), Eric Goldsmith (AOL), and two posts from Ara Pehlivanian (Yahoo!).

The articles were warmly accepted by the community and then the following year, in December 2010, the calendar was already something people were looking forward to reading. The calendar also got a new home at *http://calendar.perfplanet.com* as a subdomain of the "Planet Performance" feed aggregator. And this time around more people were willing to help. Developers of all around our industry were willing to contribute their time, to share and spread their knowledge, announce new tools, and this way create a much better set of 24 articles than a single person could. This is what soon will become Volume 1 of the series of Daybooks.

Then came December 2011, and we had so much good content and enthusiasm that we kept going past December 24, all the way to December 31, even publishing two articles on the last day. This is the content that you have in your hands in a book format as *Web Performance Daybook, Volume 2.*

Our WPO community is young, small, but growing, and in need of nourishment in the form of community building events such as the advent calendar. That's why it was exciting to have the opportunity to collaborate on this title with O'Reilly and all 32 authors. I'm really happy with the result and I know that both volumes will serve as a reference and introduction to performance tools, research, techniques, and approaches for years to come. There's always the risk with outdated content in offline technical publications, but I see references to the calendar articles in the latest conferences today all the time, so I'm confident this knowledge is to remain fresh for quite a while and some of it is even destined to become timeless.

Enjoy the book, prepare to learn from the brightest in the industry and, most of all, be ready to make the Web a better place for all of us!

—Stoyan Stefanov

About the Authors

Patrick Meenan

Patrick Meenan (*http://blog.patrickmeenan.com/*) (@patmeenan) created WebPagetest (*http://www.webpagetest .org/*) while working at AOL and now works at Google with the team that is working to make the Web faster (*http://code.google .com/speed/*).

Nicholas Zakas

Nicholas C. Zakas (*http://www.nczonline.net/*) (@slicknet) is chief architect of WellFurnished, a site dedicated to helping you find beautiful home decor. Prior to that, he worked at Yahoo! for almost five years, where he was a presentation architect, frontend lead for the Yahoo! homepage, and a contributor to the YUI library. He is the author of *Maintainable JavaScript* (O'Reilly, 2012), *Professional JavaScript for Web Developers* (Wrox, 2012), *Professional Ajax* (Wrox, 2007), and *High Performance Java-Script* (O'Reilly, 2010). Nicholas is a strong advocate for development best practices including progressive enhancement, accessibility, performance, scalability, and maintainability. He blogs regularly at *http://www.nczonline.net/*.

Guy Podjarny

Guy Podjarny (*http://blaze.io/*) (@guypod) is Web Performance and Security expert, specializing in Mobile Web Performance, CTO at Blaze. Guy spent the last decade prior to Blaze as a Software Architect and Web Application Security expert, driving the IBM Rational AppScan product line from inception to being the leading Web Application Security assessment tool. Guy has filed over 15 patents, presented at numerous conferences, and has published several professional papers.

Stoyan Stefanov

Stoyan Stefanov (*http://phpied.com/*) (@stoyanstefanov) is a Facebook engineer, former Yahoo! writer ("JavaScript Patterns", "Object-Oriented JavaScript"), speaker (JSConf, Velocity, Fronteers), toolmaker (Smush.it, YSlow 2.0), and a Guitar Hero wannabe (*http://givepngachance.com/*).

Tim Kadlec

Tim Kadlec (*http://timkadlec.com*) (@tkadlec) is web developer living and working in northern Wisconsin. His diverse background working with small companies to large publishers and industrial corporations has allowed him to see how the careful application of web technologies can impact businesses of all sizes.

Tim organizes Breaking Development (*http://bdconf.com*), a biannual conference dedicated to web design and development for mobile devices.

He is currently writing a book entitled *Implementing Responsive Design: Building Sites for an Anywhere, Everywhere Web* (*http://responsiveenhancement.com*), due out in the fall of 2012.

Brian Pane

Brian Pane (*http://www.brianp.net/*) (@brianpane) is an Internet technology and product generalist. He has worked at companies including Disney, CNET, F5, and Facebook; and all along the way he's jumped at any opportunity to make software faster.

Josh Fraser

Josh Fraser (*http://onlineaspect.com/*) (@joshfraser) is the co-founder and CEO of Torbit, a company that automates front-end optimizations that are proven to increase the speed of your website. Josh graduated from Clemson University with a BS in computer science and previously founded a company called EventVue. He currently lives in Mountain View and is obsessed with speed.

Steve Souders

Steve Souders (*http://stevesouders.com/*) (@souders) works at Google (*http://www.google.com/*) on web performance and open source initiatives. His book, *High Performance Web Sites*, explains his best practices for performance; it was #1 in Amazon's Computer and Internet bestsellers. His follow-up book, *Even Faster Web Sites*, provides performance tips for today's Web 2.0 applications. Steve is the creator of YSlow, the performance analysis extension to Firebug, with over 2 million downloads. He also created Cuzillion, SpriteMe, and Browserscope. He serves as co-chair of Velocity, the web performance and operations conference from O'Reilly, and is co-founder of the Firebug Working Group. He taught CS193H: High Performance Web Sites at Stanford, and frequently speaks at conferences including OSCON, The Ajax Experience, SXSW, and Web 2.0 Expo.

Betty Tso

Betty is a Software Development Manager at Amazon. Prior to that, she led the Exceptional Performance Engineering team at Yahoo! and drove the engineering execution and development for Yahoo!'s top Web Performance products like YSlow and Roundtrip.

Betty is also an evangelist in the Web Performance Optimization domain. She has spoken at Velocity Conferences, the Yahoo! Frontend Summit, and universities such as Georgia Tech, Duke, UIUC, University of Texas at Austin, and UCSD. She was also co-President of Yahoo! Women-in-Tech, a 600+ members organization that empowers women to succeed in their career, foster employee growth, and inspire young girls to pursue technical careers.

Israel Nir

Israel Nir (@shunra) likes to create stuff, break other stuff apart, code, the number 0x17, and playing the ukulele. He also works as a team leader at Shunra, where he builds tools to make applications run faster.

Marcel Duran

Marcel Duran (*http://javascriptrules.com/*) is currently a Front End Engineer at Twitter, Inc. Prior to that, he was into web performance optimization on high traffic sites at Yahoo! Front Page and Search teams where he applied and researched web performance best practices making pages even faster. On his last role as the Front End Lead for Yahoo!'s Exceptional Performance Team, he was dedicated to YSlow (now as his personal open source project) and other performance tools development, researches, and evangelism.

Éric Daspet

Éric Daspet (*http://eric.daspet.name/*) (@edasfr) is a web consultant in France. He wrote about PHP, founded Paris-Web conferences to promote web quality, and is now pushing performance with a local user group and a future book.

Alois Reitbauer

Alois Reitbauer (*http://blog.dynatrace.com/*) (@aloisreitbauer) works as Technology Strategist for dynaTrace software and heads the dynaTrace Center of Excellence. As a major contributor to dynaTrace Labs technology he influences the companies future technological direction. Besides his engineering work, he supports Fortune 500 companies in implementing successful performance management.

Matthew Prince

Matthew Prince (*http://www.cloudflare.com/*) (@eastdakota) is the co-founder & CEO of CloudFlare. Matthew wrote his first computer program when he was 7, and hasn't been able to shake the bug since. After attending the University of Chicago Law School, he worked as an attorney for one day before jumping at the opportunity to be a founding member of a tech startup. He hasn't looked back. CloudFlare is Matthew's third entrepreneurial venture. On the side, Matthew teaches Internet law as an adjunct professor, is a certified ski instructor and regular attendee of the Sundance Film Festival.

Buddy Brewer

Buddy Brewer (@bbrewer) is a co-founder of Log Normal, a company that shows you exactly how much time real people spend waiting on your website. He has worked on web performance issues in various roles for almost ten years.

Alexander Podelko

The last fourteen years Alex Podelko (*http://alexanderpodelko .com/blog/*) (@apodelko) worked as a performance engineer and architect for several companies. Currently he is Consulting Member of Technical Staff at Oracle, responsible for performance testing and optimization of Hyperion products. Alex currently serves as a director for the Computer Measurement Group (CMG). He maintains a collection of performance-related links and documents.

Estelle Weyl

Estelle Weyl (*http://www.standardista.com/*) (@estellevw) started her professional life in architecture, then managed teen health programs. In 2000, she took the natural step of becoming a web standardista. She has consulted for Kodakgallery, Yahoo! and Apple, among others. Estelle provides tutorials and detailed grids of CSS3 and HTML5 browser support in her blog. She is the author of Mobile HTML5 (*http://oreilly.com/catalog/ 9780980846904*) (O'Reilly, Oct. 2011) and *HTML5 and CSS3 for the Real World* (Sitepoint, May 2011). While not coding, she works in construction, de-hippifying her 1960s throwback abode.

Aaron Peters

Aaron Peters (*http://www.aaronpeters.nl/en/*) (@aaronpeters) is an independent web performance consultant based in The Netherlands. He is a Red Hot Chili Peppers fan and will kick your butt in a snowboard contest anytime.

Tony Gentilcore

Tony Gentilcore (@tonygentilcore) is a software engineer at Google. He enjoys making the Web faster and has recently added support for Web Timing and async scripts to Google Chrome/ WebKit.

Matthew Steele

Matthew Steele is a software engineer at Google, working on making the Web faster. Matthew has worked on Page Speed for Firefox and Chrome, has contributed to mod_pagespeed, and most recently, has led design and development of mod_spdy for Apache.

Bryan McQuade

Bryan McQuade (@bryanmcquade) leads the Page Speed team at Google. He has contributed to various projects that make the Web faster, including Shared Dictionary Compression over HTTP and optimizing web servers to better utilize HTTP.

Tobie Langel

Tobie Langel (*http://tobielangel.com/*) (@tobie) is a Software engineer at Facebook. He's also Facebook's W3C AC Rep. An avid open-source contributor (*https://github.com/tobie*), he's mostly known for having co-maintained the Prototype JavaScript Framework. Tobie recently picked up blogging again and rants at blog.tobie.me (*http://blog.tobie.me/*). In a previous life, he was a professional jazz drummer.

Billy Hoffman

If there is one thing Billy Hoffman believes in, it's transparency. In fact, he once got sued over it, but that is another story. Billy continues to push for transparency as founder and CEO of Zoompf, whose products provide visibility into your website's performance by identifying the specific issues that are slowing your site down. You can follow Zoompf on Twitter (*http://twitter .com/zoompf*) and read Billy's performance research on Zoompf's blog Lickity Split (*http://zoompf.com/blog*).

Joshua Bixby

Joshua Bixby (@JoshuaBixby) is president of Strangeloop (*http://www.strangeloopnetworks.com/*), which provides website acceleration solutions to companies like eBay/PayPal, Visa, Petco, Wine.com, and O'Reilly Media. Joshua also maintains the blog Web Performance Today (*http://www.webperformancetoday.com/*), which explores issues and ideas about site speed, user behavior, and performance optimization.

Sergey Chernyshev

Sergey Chernyshev (*http://www.sergeychernyshev.com/*) (@sergeyche) organizes New York Web Performance Meetup and helps other performance enthusiasts around the world start meetups in their cities. Sergey volunteers his time to run @perfplanet (*http://twitter.com/perfplanet*) Twitter companion to Perf-Planet site. He is also an open source developer and author of a few web performance-related tools including ShowSlow, SVN Assets, drop-in .htaccess, and more.

JP Castro

JP Castro (@jphpsf) is a frontend engineer living in San Francisco. He's passionate about web development and specifically web performance. He blogs at *http://blog.jphpsf.com* and co-organizes the San Francisco performance meetup. When he's not talking about performance, he enjoys spending time with his family, being outdoors, sipping craft beers, consuming a full jar of Nutella, and playing video games.

Pavel Paulau

Pavel Paulau (@pavelpaulau) is a performance engineer from Minsk, Belarus. Besides his daily work at Couchbase (*http://www.couchbase.com*), he tries to spread importance of speed as co-author of the WebPerformance.ru blog (*http://webperformance.ru/*).

David Calhoun

David Calhoun (@franksvalli) is an independent frontend developer who has been splitting his time between California and Japan. He's the community news writer for JSMag and keeps a blog (*http://davidbcalhoun.com/*) with developer and general life thoughts (hard to put that philosophy degree to use...).

David specializes in mobile, frontend performance, and sure enough, mobile performance. He formerly worked for Yahoo! Mobile, CBSi/CNET, occasionally contracts for WebMocha, and is currently contracting at Skybox Imaging, working on interfaces for flying satellites from browsers.

Nicole Sullivan

Nicole Sullivan (*http://stubbornella.org/*) (@stubbornella) is an evangelist, frontend performance consultant, CSS Ninja, and author. She started the Object-Oriented CSS open source project, which answers the question: how do you scale CSS for millions of visitors or thousands of pages? She also consulted with the W3C for their beta redesign, and is the co-creator of Smush.it, an image optimization service in the cloud.

Nicole is passionate about CSS, web standards, and scalable frontend architecture for large commercial websites. She speaks about performance at conferences around the world, most recently at The Ajax Experience, ParisWeb, and Web Directions North. She co-authored *Even Faster Websites* and blogs at stubbornella.org.

James Pearce

James (*http://tripleodeon.com/*) (@jamespearce) is Head of Mobile Developer Relations at Facebook. He lives in California and in airports around the world.

Tom Hughes-Croucher

Tom (*http://tomhughescroucher.com/*) (@sh1mmer) is the principal consultant at Jetpacks for Dinosaurs, which helps make websites really rather fast. Tom consults with clients like Walmart and MySpace to name a few. An industry veteran, Tom has worked for the likes of Yahoo!, Joyent, NASA, Tesco, and many more. Tom co-authored *Up and Running with Node.js* (*http://shop.oreilly.com/product/0636920015956.do*) and lives in San Francisco, CA.

Dave Artz

David Artz leads the Site Engineering team at AOL. He led AOL's Optimization team in the past—a team focused on setting standards and developing best practices in frontend engineering, performance, and SEO across the teams he now leads. While managing multiple teams, he has continued to develop script/CSS/font loaders as part of his Boot library (*https://github.com/artzstudio/Boot*), an AMD loader for jQuery (*https://github.com/artzstudio/jQuery-AMD*), and a jQuery plug-in called Sonar (*https://github.com/artzstudio/jQuery-Sonar*) for easily loading content and functionality in on demand using special "*scrollin*" and "*scrollout*" events.

Preface

Conventions Used in This Book

The following typographical conventions are used in this book:

Italic

> Indicates new terms, URLs, email addresses, filenames, and file extensions.

`Constant width`

> Used for program listings, as well as within paragraphs to refer to program elements such as variable or function names, databases, data types, environment variables, statements, and keywords.

`Constant width bold`

> Shows commands or other text that should be typed literally by the user.

`Constant width italic`

> Shows text that should be replaced with user-supplied values or by values determined by context.

 This icon signifies a tip, suggestion, or general note.

 This icon indicates a warning or caution.

Using Code Examples

This book is here to help you get your job done. In general, you may use the code in this book in your programs and documentation. You do not need to contact us for permission unless you're reproducing a significant portion of the code. For example, writing a program that uses several chunks of code from this book does not require permission. Selling or distributing a CD-ROM of examples from O'Reilly books does require permission. Answering a question by citing this book and quoting example code does not require permission. Incorporating a significant amount of example code from this book into your product's documentation does require permission.

We appreciate, but do not require, attribution. An attribution usually includes the title, author, publisher, and ISBN. For example: "*Web Performance Daybook, Volume Two* edited by Stoyan Stefanov (O'Reilly). Copyright 2012 Stoyan Stefanov, 978-1-449-33291-4."

If you feel your use of code examples falls outside fair use or the permission given above, feel free to contact us at *permissions@oreilly.com*.

Safari® Books Online

Safari Books Online (*www.safaribooksonline.com*) is an on-demand digital library that delivers expert content in both book and video form from the world's leading authors in technology and business.

Technology professionals, software developers, web designers, and business and creative professionals use Safari Books Online as their primary resource for research, problem solving, learning, and certification training.

Safari Books Online offers a range of product mixes and pricing programs for organizations, government agencies, and individuals. Subscribers have access to thousands of books, training videos, and prepublication manuscripts in one fully searchable database from publishers like O'Reilly Media, Prentice Hall Professional, Addison-Wesley Professional, Microsoft Press, Sams, Que, Peachpit Press, Focal Press, Cisco Press, John Wiley & Sons, Syngress, Morgan Kaufmann, IBM Redbooks, Packt, Adobe Press, FT Press, Apress, Manning, New Riders, McGraw-Hill, Jones & Bartlett, Course Technology, and dozens more. For more information about Safari Books Online, please visit us online.

How to Contact Us

Please address comments and questions concerning this book to the publisher:

O'Reilly Media, Inc.
1005 Gravenstein Highway North
Sebastopol, CA 95472
800-998-9938 (in the United States or Canada)
707-829-0515 (international or local)
707-829-0104 (fax)

We have a web page for this book, where we list errata, examples, and any additional information. You can access this page at:

http://oreil.ly/web_perf_daybook_v2

To comment or ask technical questions about this book, send email to:

bookquestions@oreilly.com

For more information about our books, courses, conferences, and news, see our website at *http://www.oreilly.com*.

Find us on Facebook: *http://facebook.com/oreilly*

Follow us on Twitter: *http://twitter.com/oreillymedia*

Watch us on YouTube: *http://www.youtube.com/oreillymedia*

CHAPTER 1

WebPagetest Internals

Patrick Meenan

I thought I'd take the opportunity this year to give a little bit of visibility into how WebPagetest (*http://www.webpagetest.org/*) gathers the performance data from browsers. Other tools on windows use similar techniques but the information here may not be representative of how other tools work.

First off, it helps to understand the networking stack on Windows from a browser's perspective (Figure 1-1).

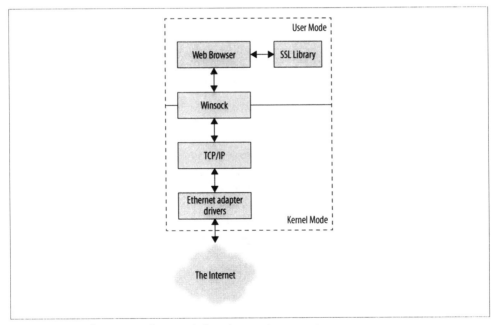

Figure 1-1. Windows networking stack from browser's perspective

It doesn't matter what the browser is, if it runs on Windows, the architecture pretty much *has* to look like the diagram above where all of the communications go through the Windows socket APIs (for that matter, just about any application that talks TCP/IP on Windows looks like the picture above).

Function Interception

The key to how WebPagetest works is its ability to intercept arbitrary function calls and inspect or alter the request or response before passing it on to the original implementation (or choosing not to pass it on at all). Luckily someone else did most of the heavy lifting and provided a nice open source library (*http://newgre.net/ncodehook*) that can take care of the details for you but it basically works like this:

- Find the target function in memory (trivial if it is exported from a dll).
- Copy the first several bytes from the function (making sure to keep x86 instructions intact).
- Overwrite the function entry with a jmp to the new function.
- Provide a replacement function that includes the bytes copied from the original function along with a jmp to the remaining code.

It's pretty hairy stuff and things tend to go *very* wrong if you aren't extremely careful, but with well-defined functions (like all of the Windows APIs), you can pretty much intercept anything you'd like.

One catch is that you can only redirect calls to code running in the same process as the original function, which is fine if you wrote the code but doesn't help a lot if you are trying to spy on software that you don't control which leads us to...

Code Injection

Lucky for me, Windows provides several ways to inject arbitrary code into processes. There is a good overview of several different techniques here: *http://www.codeproject.com/KB/threads/winspy.aspx*, and there are actually more ways to do it than that but it covers the basics. Some of the techniques insert your code into every process but I wanted to be a lot more targeted and just instrument the specific browser instances that we are interested in, so after a bunch of experimentation (and horrible failures), I ended up using the CreateRemoteThread/LoadLibrary technique which essentially lets you force any process to load an arbitrary dll and execute code in it (assuming you have the necessary rights).

Resulting Browser Architecture

Now that we can intercept arbitrary function calls, it just becomes a matter of identifying the "interesting" functions, preferably ones that are used by all the browsers so you can reuse as much code as possible. In WebPagetest, we intercept all the Winsock calls that have to do with resolving host names, connecting sockets, and reading or writing data (Figure 1-2).

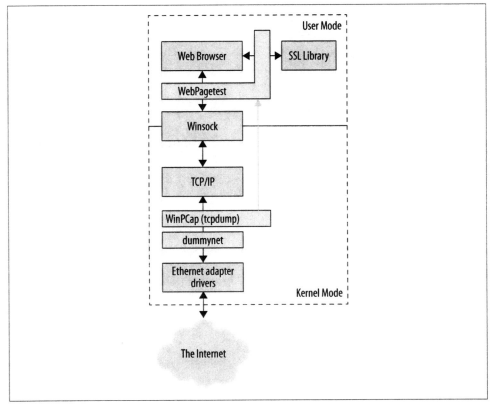

Figure 1-2. Browser architecture

This gives us access to all the network access from the browser and we essentially just keep track of what the browsers are doing. Other than having to decode the raw byte streams, it is pretty straightforward and gives us a consistent way to do the measurements across all browsers. SSL does add a bit of a wrinkle so we also intercept calls to the various SSL libraries that the browsers use in order that we can see the unencrypted version of the data. This is a little more difficult for Chrome since the library is compiled into the Chrome code itself, but luckily they make debug symbols available for every build so we can still find the code in memory.

The same technique is used to intercept drawing calls from the browser so we can tell when it paints to the screen (for the start render measurement).

Get the Code

Since WebPagetest is under a BSD license you are welcome to reuse any of the code for whatever purposes you'd like. The project lives on Google Code here: (*http://code.goo gle.com/p/webpagetest/*) and some of the more interesting files are:

- Winsock API interception code (*http://webpagetest.googlecode.com/svn/trunk/ agent/wpthook/hook_winsock.cc*)
- Code injection (*http://webpagetest.googlecode.com/svn/trunk/agent/wpthook/inject .cc*)

Browser Advancements

Luckily, browsers are starting to expose more interesting information in standard ways and as the W3C Resource Timing spec (*http://w3c-test.org/webperf/specs/ResourceTim ing/*) advances, you will be able to access a lot of this information directly from the browser through JavaScript (even from your end users!).

 To comment on this chapter, please visit *http://calendar.perfplanet.com/ 2011/webpagetest-internals/*. Originally published on Dec 01, 2011.

localStorage Read Performance

Nicholas Zakas

Web Storage (*http://dev.w3.org/html5/webstorage/*) has quickly become one of the most popular HTML5-related additions to the web developer toolkit. More specifically, `localStorage` has found a home in the hearts and minds of web developers everywhere, providing very quick and easy client-side data storage that persists across sessions. With a simple key-value interface, we've seen sites take advantage of `localStorage` in unique and interesting ways:

- Disqus (*http://www.disqus.com/*), the popular feedback management system, uses `localStorage` to save your comment as you type. So if something horrible happens, you can fire back up the browser and pick up where you left off.
- Google (*http://www.google.com/*) and Bing (*http://www.bing.com/*) store JavaScript and CSS in `localStorage` to improve their mobile site performance (more info: *http://www.stevesouders.com/blog/2011/03/28/storager-case-study-bing-google/*).

Of the use cases I've seen, the Google/Bing approach is one that seems to be gaining in popularity. This is partly due to the difficulties of working with the HTML5 application cache and partly due to the publicity that this technique has gained from the work of Steve Souders and others. Indeed, the more I talk to people about `localStorage` and how useful it can be for storing UI-related information, the more people I find who have already started to experiment with this technique.

What I find intriguing about this use of `localStorage` is that there's a built-in, and yet unstated, assumption: that reading from `localStorage` is an inexpensive operation. I had heard anecdotally from other developers about strange performance issues, and so I set out to quantify the performance characteristics of `localStorage`, to determine the actual cost of reading data.

The Benchmark

Not too long ago, I created and shared a simple benchmark that measured reading a value from `localStorage` against reading a value from an object property. Several others tweaked the benchmark to arrive at a more reliable version (*http://jsperf.com/localstor age-vs-objects/10*). The end result: reading from `localStorage` is orders of magnitude slower *in every browser* than reading the same data from an object property. Exactly how much slower? Take a look at the chart on Figure 2-1 (higher numbers are better).

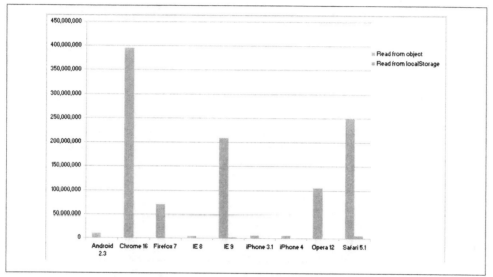

Figure 2-1. Benchmark results

You may be confused after looking at this chart because it appears that reading from `localStorage` isn't represented. In fact, it is represented, you just can't see it because *the numbers are so low as to not even be visible with this scale*. With the exception of Safari 5, whose `localStorage` readings actually show up, every other browser has such a large difference that there's no way to see it on this chart. When I adjust the Y-axis values, you can now see how the measurements stack up across browsers:

By changing the scale of the Y-axis, you're now able to see a true comparison of `local Storage` versus object property reads (Figure 2-2). But still, the difference between the two is so vast that it's almost comical. Why?

What's Going On?

In order to persist across browser sessions, values in `localStorage` are written to disk. That means when you're reading a value from `localStorage`, you're actually reading some bytes from the hard drive. Reading from and writing to a hard drive are expensive

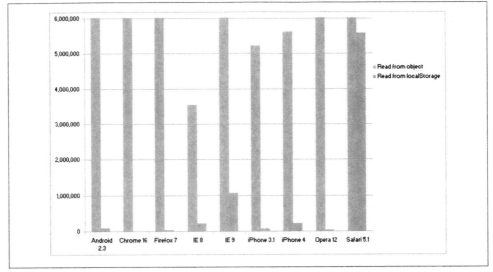

Figure 2-2. Scaled results

operations, especially as compared to reading from and writing to memory. In essence, that's exactly what my benchmark was testing: the speed of reading a value from memory (object property) compared to reading a value from disk (localStorage).

Making matters more interesting is the fact that localStorage data is stored per-origin, which means that it's possible for two or more tabs in a browser to be accessing the same localStorage data at the same time. This is a big pain for browser implementors who need to figure out how to synchronize access across tabs. When you attempt to read from localStorage, the browser needs to stop and see if any other tab is accessing the same area first. If so, it must wait until the access is finished before the value can be read.

So the delay associated with reading from localStorage is variable—it depends a lot on what else is going on with the browser at that point in time.

Optimization Strategy

Given that there is a cost to reading from localStorage, how does that affect how you would use it? Before coming to a conclusion, I ran another benchmark (*http://jsperf .com/localstorage-string-size*) to determine the effect of reading different-sized pieces of data from localStorage. The benchmarks saves four different size strings, 100 characters, 500 characters, 1,000 characters, and 2,000 characters, into localStorage and then reads them out. The results were a little surprising: across all browsers, the amount of data being read *did not* affect how quickly the read happened.

I ran the test multiple times and implored my Twitter followers (*https://twitter.com/ slicknet/status/139475625793699840*) to get more information. To be certain, there were definitely a few variances across browsers, but none that were large enough that it really makes a difference. My conclusion: it doesn't matter how much data you read from a single localStorage key.

I followed up with another benchmark (*http://jsperf.com/localstorage-string-size-re trieval*) to test my new conclusion that it's better to do as few reads as possible. The results correlated with the earlier benchmark in that reading 100 characters 10 times was around 90% slower across most browsers than reading 10,000 characters one time.

Given that, the best strategy for reading data from localStorage is to use as few keys as possible to store as much data as possible. Since it takes roughly the same amount of time to read 10 characters as it does to read 2,000 characters, try to put as much data as possible into a single value. You're getting hit each time you call getItem() (or read from a localStorage property), so make sure that you're getting the most out of the expense. The faster you get data into memory, either a variable or an object property, the faster all subsequent actions.

Follow Up

In the time since I first published this article, there has been a lot of discussion around localStorage performance. It began with a blog post by Mozilla's Chris Heilmann titled, "There's No Simple Solution for localStorage." (*http://hacks.mozilla.org/2012/03/there -is-no-simple-solution-for-local-storage/*) In that post, Chris introduced the idea that localStorage as a whole has performance problems. After several follow up blog posts by others, including myself, I was finally able to get in touch with Jonas Sicking, one of the engineers responsible for implementing localStorage in Firefox. Indeed, there is a performance issue with localStorage, but it's not as simple as reads taking a bit longer than reads on the simple object. The heart of the problem is that localStorage is a synchronous API, which leaves the browser with very few choices as to implementation. All localStorage data is stored in a file on disk. That means in order for you to have access to that data in JavaScript the browser must first read that file into memory. When that read occurs is the performance issue. It could occur with the first access of local Storage, but then the browser would freeze while the read happened. That may not be a big deal when dealing with a small amount of data, but if you've used the whole 5 MB limit, there could be a noticeable effect. Another solution, the one employed by Firefox, is to read the localStorage data file as a page is being loaded. This ensures that later access to localStorage is as fast as possible and has predictable performance. The downside of that approach is that the read from file could adversely affect the loading time of the page. As I'm writing this, there is still no solution to this particular problem. Some are calling for a completely new API to replace localStorage while others are intent on fixing the existing API. Regardless of what happens, there is likely to be a lot more research done in the area of client-side data storage soon.

To comment on this chapter, please visit *http://calendar.perfplanet.com/ 2011/localstorage-read-performance/*. Originally published on Dec 02, 2011.

CHAPTER 3

Why Inlining Everything Is NOT the Answer

Guy Podjarny

Every so often I get asked if the best frontend optimization wouldn't be to simply inline everything. Inlining everything means embedding all the scripts, styles, and images into the HTML, and serving them as one big package.

This question is a great example of taking a best practice too far. Yes, reducing the number of HTTP requests is a valuable best practice. Yes, inlining everything is the ultimate way to reduce the number of requests (in theory to one). But NO, it's not the best way to make your site faster.

While reducing requests is a good practice, it's not the only aspect that matters. If you inline everything, you fulfill the "Reduce Requests" goal, but you're missing many others. Here are some of the specific reasons you shouldn't inline everything.

No Browser Caching

The most obvious problem with inlining everything is the loss of caching. If the HTML holds all the resources, and the HTML is not cacheable by itself, the resources are re-downloaded every time. This means the first page load on a new site may be faster, but subsequent pages or return visitors would experience a slower page load.

For example, let's look at the repeat visit of the *New York Times*' home page (Table 3-1, Figure 3-1). Thanks to caching, the original site loads in 2.7 seconds. If we inline the JavaScript files on that page, the repeat visit load time climbs to 3.2 seconds, and the size doubles. Visually, the negative impact is much greater, due to JavaScript's impact on rendering.

Table 3-1. www.nyt.com IE8; DSL; Dulles, VA

Repeat view	Load time	# Request	# Bytes
Original Site	2.701 seconds	46	101 KB
Inlined External JS Files	3.159 seconds	36	212 KB

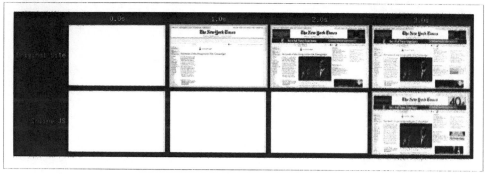

Figure 3-1. www.nyt.com

Even if the HTML is cacheable, the cache duration has to be the shortest duration of all the resources on the page. If your HTML is cacheable for 10 minutes, and a resource in the page is cacheable for a day, you're effectively reducing the cacheability of the resource to be 10 minutes as well.

No Edge Caching

The traditional value of CDNs is called Edge Caching: caching static resources on the CDN edge. Cached resources are served directly from the edge, and thus delivered much faster than routing all the way to the origin server to get them.

When inlining data, the resources are bundled into the HTML, and from the CDN's perspective, the whole thing is just one HTTP response. If the HTML is not cacheable, this entire HTTP response isn't cacheable either. Therefore, the HTML and all of its resources would need to be fetched from the origin every time a user requests the page, while in the standard case many of the resources could have been served from the Edge Cache.

As a result, even first-time visitors to your site are likely to get a slower experience from a page with inlined resources than from a page with linked resources. This is especially true when the client is browsing from a location far from your server.

For example, let's take a look at browsing the Apple home page from Brazil, using IE8 and a cable connection. (Table 3-2, Figure 3-2) Modifying the site to inline images increased the load time from about 2.4s to about 3.1s, likely since the inlined image data had to be fetched from the original servers and not the CDN. While the number of requests decreased by 30%, the page was in fact slower.

Table 3-2. www.apple.com IE8; Cable; Sao Paolo, Brazil

First view	Load time	# Request	# Bytes
Original Site	2.441 seconds	36	363 KB
Inlined Images	3.157 seconds	26	361 KB

Figure 3-2. www.apple.com

No Loading On-Demand

Loading resources on-demand is an important category of performance optimizations, which attempt to only load a resource when it's actually required. Resources may be referenced, but not actually downloaded and evaluated until the conditions require it.

Browsers offer a built-in loading-on-demand mechanism for CSS images. If a CSS rule references a background image, the browser would only download it if at least one element on the page matched the rule. Another example is loading images on-demand (*http://www.blaze.io/technical/the-impact-of-image-optimization/*), which only downloads page images as they scroll into view. The Progressive Enhancement approach to Mobile Web Design uses similar concepts for loading JavaScript and CSS only as needed.

Since inlining resources is a decision made on the server, it doesn't benefit from loading on-demand. This means all the images (CSS or page images) are embedded, whether they're needed by the specific client context or not. More often than not, the value gained by inlining is lower than the value lost by not having these other optimizations.

As an example, I took *The Sun*'s home page and applied two conflicting optimizations to it (Table 3-3, Figure 3-3). The first loads images on demand, and the second inlines all images. When loading images on demand, the page size added up to about 1MB, and load time was around 9 seconds. When inlining images, the page size grew to almost 2MB, and the load time increased to 16 seconds. Either way the page makes many requests, but the load and size differences between inlining images and images on-demand are very noticeable.

Table 3-3. *www.thesun.co.uk IE8; DSL; Dulles, VA*

First view	Load time	# Request	# Bytes
Loading Images On-Demand	9.038 seconds	194	1,028 KB
Inlined Images	16.190 seconds	228	1,979 KB

Figure 3-3. *www.thesun.co.uk*

Invalidates Browser Look-Ahead

Modern browsers use smart heuristics to try and prefetch resources at the bottom of the page ahead of time. For instance, if your site references *http://www.3rdparty.com/ code.js* towards the end of the HTML, the browser is likely to resolve the DNS for *www. 3rdparty.com*, and probably even start downloading the file, long before it can actually execute it.

In a standard website, the HTML itself is small, and so the browser only needs to download a few dozen KB before it sees the entire HTML. Once it sees (and parses) the entire HTML, it can start prefetching as it sees fit. If you're making heavy use of inlining, the HTML itself becomes much bigger, possibly over 0.5MB in size. While downloading it, the browser can't see and accelerate the resources further down the page—many of which are third-party tools you couldn't inline.

Flawed Solution: Inline Everything only on First Visit

A partial solution to the caching problem works as follows:

- The first time a user visits your site, inline everything and set a cookie for the user
- Once the page loads, download all the resources as individual files.
  - —Or store the data into a Scriptable Cache (*http://www.blaze.io/technical/ browser-cache-2-0-scriptable-cache/*)
- If a user visits the page and has the cookie, assume it has the files in the cache, and don't inline the data.

While better than nothing, the flaw in this solution is that it assumes a page is either entirely cached or entirely not cached. In reality, websites and cache states are extremely volatile. A user's cache can only hold less than a day's worth of browsing data: An average user browses 88 pages/day (*http://blog.newrelic.com/wp-content/uploads/infog _061611.png*), an average page weighs 930KB (*http://httparchive.org/interesting.php #bytesperpage*), and most desktop browsers cache no more than 75MB of data (*http:// www.blaze.io/mobile/understanding-mobile-cache-sizes/*). For mobile, the ratio is even worse.

Cookies, on the other hand, usually live until their defined expiry date. Therefore, using a cookie to predict the cache state becomes pointless very quickly, and then you're just back to not inlining at all.

One of the biggest problems with this solution is that it demos better than it really is. In synthetic testing, like WebPageTest tests, a page is indeed either fully cached (i.e., all its resources are cached), or it's not cached at all. These tests therefore make the inline-on-first-visit approach look like the be all and end all, which is just plain wrong.

Another significant problem is that not all CDNs support varying cache by a cookie. Therefore, if some of your pages are cacheable, or if you think you might make them cacheable later, it may be hard to impossible to get the CDN to cache two different versions of your page, and choose the one to serve based on a cookie.

Summary and Recommendations

Our world isn't black and white. The fact that reducing the number of requests is a good way to accelerate your site doesn't mean it's the only solution. If you take it too far, you'll end up slowing down your site, not speeding it up.

Despite all these limitations, inlining is still a good and important tool in the world of frontend Optimization. As such, you should use it, but be careful not to abuse it. Here are some recommendations about when to use inlining, but keep in mind you should verify that they get the right effect on your own site:

Very small files should be inlined.
> The HTTP overhead of a request and response is often ~1KB, so files smaller than that should definitely be inlined. Our testing shows you should almost never inline files bigger than 4KB.

Page images (i.e., images referenced from the page, not CSS) should rarely be inlined.
> Page images tend to be big in size, they don't block other resources in the normal use, and they tend to change more frequently than CSS and Scripts. To optimize image file loading, load images on-demand instead (*http://www.blaze.io/technical/ the-impact-of-image-optimization/*).

Anything that isn't critical for the above-the-fold page view should not be inlined.
> Instead, it should be deferred till after page load, or at least made async.

Be careful with inlining CSS images.

Many CSS files are shared across many pages, where each page only uses a third or less of the rules. If that's the case for your site, there's a decent chance your site will be faster if you don't inline those images.

Don't rely only on synthetic measurements—use RUM (Real User Monitoring).

Tools like WebPageTest are priceless, but they don't show everything. Measure real world performance and use that information alongside your synthetic test results.

 To comment on this chapter, please visit *http://calendar.perfplanet.com/ 2011/why-inlining-everything-is-not-the-answer/*. Originally published on Dec 03, 2011.

CHAPTER 4

The Art and Craft of the Async Snippet

Stoyan Stefanov

JavaScript downloads block the loading of other page components. That's why it's important (make that *critical*) to load script files in a nonblocking asynchronous fashion. If this is new to you, you can start with this post on the Yahoo User Interface (YUI) library blog (*http://www.yuiblog.com/blog/2008/07/22/non-blocking-scripts/*) or the Performance Calendar article (*http://calendar.perfplanet.com/2010/the-truth-about-non-blocking-javascript/*).

In this post, I'll examine the topic from the perspective of a third party—when you're the third party, providing a snippet for other developers to include on their pages. Be it an ad, a plug-in, widget, visits counter, analytics, or anything else.

Let's see in much detail how this issue is addressed in Facebook's JavaScript SDK.

The Facebook Plug-ins JS SDK

The Facebook JavaScript SDK (*https://developers.facebook.com/docs/reference/java script/*) is a multipurpose piece of code that lets you integrate Facebook services, make API calls, and load social plug-ins such as the Like button (*https://developers.facebook .com/docs/reference/plugins/like/*).

The task of the SDK when it comes to Like button and other social plug-ins is to parse the page's HTML code looking for elements (such as `<fb:like>` or `<div class="fb-like">`) to replace with a plug-in. The plug-in itself is an iframe that points to something like `facebook.com/plugins/like.php` with the appropriate URL parameters and appropriately sized.

This is an example of one such plug-in URL:

```
https://www.facebook.com/plugins/like.php?href=bookofspeed.com&lay
out=box_count
```

The JavaScript SDK has a URL like so:

```
http://connect.facebook.net/en_US/all.js
```

The question is how do you include this code on your page. Traditionally it has been the simplest possible (but blocking) way:

```
<script src="http://connect.facebook.net/en_US/all.js"></script>
```

Since day one of the social plug-ins though, it has always been possible to load this script asynchronously and it was guaranteed to work. Additionally, a few months ago the async snippet became the default when SDK snippet code is being generated by the various wizard-type configurators.

Figure 4-1 shows how an example configurator looks like.

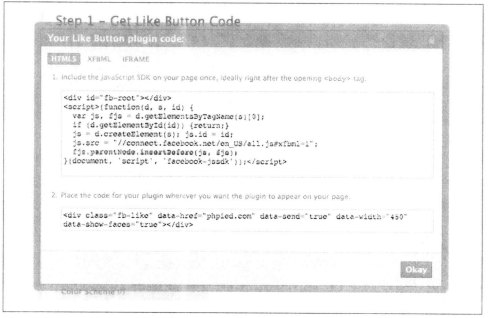

Figure 4-1. Like button configurator

The async code looks more complicated (it's longer) than the traditional one, but it's well worth it for the overall loading speed of the host page.

Before we inspect this snippet, let's see what some of the goals were when designing a third-party provider snippet.

Design Goals

- The snippet should be small. Not necessarily measured in number of bytes, but overall it shouldn't look intimidating.
- Even though it's small, it should be readable. So no minifying allowed.
- It should work in "hostile" environments. You have no control over the host page. It may be a valid XTHML-strict page, it may be missing doctype, it may even be missing (or have more than one) <body>, <head>, <html> or any other tag.
- The snippet should be copy-paste-friendly. In addition to being small that means it should just work, because people using this code may not even be developers. Or, if they are developers, they may not necessarily have the time to read documentation. That also means that some people will paste that snippet of code many times on the same page, even though the JS needs to be loaded only once per page.
- It should be unobtrusive to the host page, meaning it should leave no globals and other leftovers, other than, of course, the included JavaScript.

The Snippet

The snippet in the Facebook plug-in configurators looks like so:

```
<script>(function(d, s, id) {
  var js, fjs = d.getElementsByTagName(s)[0];
  if (d.getElementById(id)) return;
  js = d.createElement(s); js.id = id;
  js.src = "//connect.facebook.net/en_US/all.js#xfbml=1";
  fjs.parentNode.insertBefore(js, fjs);
}(document, 'script', 'facebook-jssdk'));</script>
```

Take a look at what's going on here.

On the first and last line you see that the whole snippet is wrapped in an immediate (a.k.a., self-invoking, aka self-executing) function. This is to assure that any temporary variables remain in the local scope and don't bleed into the host page's global namespace.

On line 1, you can also see that the immediate function accepts three arguments, and these are supplied on the last line when the function is invoked. These arguments are shorthands to the document object and two strings, all of which are used more than once later in the function. Passing them as arguments is somewhat shorter than defining them in the body of the function. It also saves a line (vertical space), because the other option is something like:

```
<script>(function() {
  var js, fjs = d.getElementsByTagName(s)[0],
      d = document, s = 'script', id = 'facebook-jssdk';
  // the rest...
}());</script>
```

This would be one line longer (remember we want readable snippet, not overly long lines). Also the first and the last line will have "unused" space as they are somewhat short.

Having things like the repeating `document` assigned to a shorter `d` makes the whole snippet shorter and also probably marginally faster as `d` is local which is looked up faster than the global `document`.

Next we have:

```
var js, fjs = d.getElementsByTagName(s)[0];
```

This line declares a variable and finds the first available `<script>` element on the page. I'll get to that in a second.

Line 3 checks whether the script isn't already on the page and if so, exits early as there's nothing more to do:

```
if (d.getElementById(id)) return;
```

We only need the file once. This line prevents the script file from being included several times when people copy and paste this code multiple times on the same page. This is especially bad with a regular blocking script tag because the end result is something like (assuming a blog post type of page):

```
<script src="...all.js"></script>
<fb:like /> <!-- one like button at the top of the blog post -->

<script src="...all.js"></script>
<fb:like/> <!-- second like like button at the end of the post -->

<script src="...all.js"></script>
<fb:comments/> <!-- comments plugin after the article -->

<script src="...all.js"></script>
<fb:recommendations/> <!-- sidebar with recommendations plugin -->
```

This results in a duplicate JavaScript, which is all kinds of bad (*http://developer.yahoo .com/performance/rules.html#js_dupes*), because some browsers may end up downloading the file several times.

Even if the JavaScript is asynchronous and even if the browser is smart enough not to reparse it, it will still need to re-execute it, in which case the script overwrites itself, redefining its functions and objects again and again. Highly undesirable.

So having the script with an id like `'facebook-jssdk'` which is unlikely to clash with something on the host page, lets us check if the file has already been included. If that's not the case, we move on.

The next line creates a `script` element and assigns the ID so we can check for it later:

```
js = d.createElement(s); js.id = id;
```

The following line sets the source of the script:

```
js.src = "//connect.facebook.net/en_US/all.js#xfbml=1";
```

Note that the protocol of the URL is missing. This means that the script will be loaded using the host page's protocol. If the host page uses `http://`, the script will load faster, and if the page uses `https://` there will be no mixed content security prompts.

Finally, we append the newly created `js` element to the DOM of the host page and we're done:

```
fjs.parentNode.insertBefore(js, fjs);
```

How does that work? Well, `fjs` is the first (f) JavaScript (js) element available on the page. We grabbed it earlier on line #2. We insert our new `js` element right before the `fjs`. If, let's say, the host page has a script element right after the `body`, then:

- `fjs` is the script.
- `fjs.parentNode` is the body.
- The new script is inserted between the `body` and the old `script`.

Appending Alternatives

Why the trouble with the whole `parentNode.insertBefore`? There are simpler ways to add a node to the DOM tree, like appending to the `<head>` or to the `<body>` by using `appendChild()`, however this is the way that is guaranteed to work in nearly all cases. Let's see why the others fail.

Here is a common pattern:

```
document.getElementsByTagName('head')[0].appendChild(js);
```

Or a variation if `document.head` is available in newer browsers:

```
(document.head || document.getElementsByTagName('head')[0]).appendChild(js);
```

The problem is that you don't control the markup of the host page. What if the page doesn't have a `head` element? Will the browser create that node anyways? Turns out that most of the times, yes, but there are browsers (Opera 8, Android 1) that won't create the head. A BrowserScope test by Steve Souders demonstrates this (*http://steve souders.com/tests/autohead.html*).

What about the `body`? You gotta have the body. So you should be able to do:

```
document.body.appendChild(js);
```

I created a browserscope test (*http://www.phpied.com/files/bscope/autobody.html*) and couldn't find a browser that will not create `document.body`. But there's still the lovely "Operation Aborted" error which occurs in IE7 when the async snippet script element is nested and not a direct child of the body.

Last chance:

```
document.documentElement.firstChild.appendChild(js);
```

`document.documentElement` is the HTML element and its first child must be the head. Not necessarily, as it turns out. If there's a comment following the HTML element, WebKits will give you the comment as the first child. There's an investigation with a test case that show this (*http://robert.accettura.com/blog/2009/12/12/adventures-with -document-documentelement-firstchild/*).

Whew!

Despite the possible alternatives, it appears that using the first available `script` node and `insertBefore` is the most resilient option. There's always going to be at least one `script` node, even if that's the `script` node of the snippet itself.

(Well, "always" is a strong word in web development. As @kangax (*http://twitter.com/ kangax*) pointed out once, you can have the snippet inside a `<body onload="...">` and voila—magic!—a script without a `script` node.)

What's Missing?

You may notice some things missing in this snippet that you may have seen in other code examples.

For instance there are none of:

```
js.async = true;
js.type = "text/javascript";
js.language = "JavaScript";
```

These are all defaults which don't need to take up space, so they were omitted. Exception is the `async` in some earlier Firefox versions, but the script is already nonblocking and asynchronous enough anyway.

Same goes for the `<script>` tag itself. It's an HTML5-valid bare-bones tag with no type or language attributes.

First Parties

This whole discussion was from the perspective of a third-party script provider. If you control the markup, some things might be different and easier. You can safely refer to the head because you know it's there. You don't have to check for duplicate insertions, because you're only going to insert it once. So you may end up with something much simpler, such as:

```
<script>(function(d) {
  var js = d.createElement('script');
```

```
js.src = "http://example.org/my.js";
(d.head || d.getElementsByTagName('head')[0]).appendChild(js);
}(document));</script>
```

This is all it takes when you control the host page.

Also we assumed all the time that whenever the script arrives, it just runs. But you may have different needs, for example call a specific function once the script is ready. In which case you need to listen to `js.onload` and `js.onreadystatechange` (example: *http: //www.phpied.com/javascript-include-ready-onload/*). In even more complex examples, you may want to load several scripts and guarantee their order of execution. At this point you may want to look into any of the available script loader projects such as LAB.js (*http://labjs.com/*) or head.js (*http://headjs.com/*) which are specially designed to solve these cases.

Parting Words: On the Shoulders of Giants

It's a little disturbing that we, the web developers, need to go to all these lengths to assure an asynchronous script execution (in a third-party environment or not). One day, with a few dead browsers behind us, we'll be able to simply say `script async=true` and it will just work. Meanwhile, I hope that this post will alleviate some of the pain as a resource to people who are yet to come to this problem and will hopefully save them some time.

Google AdSense folks have gone through a lot of trial and error while sharing their progress with the community, and Mathias Bynens also wrote an inspirational critique (*http://mathiasbynens.be/notes/async-analytics-snippet*) of their snippet. Steve Souders (*http://stevesouders.com/*) has done research and written about this topic, and MSN.com was probably among the first to use such a technique for loading JavaScript. There are writeups from Yahoo and many others on the topic. These are some of the giants that have helped in the search of the "perfect" snippet. Thank you!

(Psst, and if you see something that is less than perfect in the snippet, please speak up!)

 To comment on this chapter, please visit *http://calendar.perfplanet.com/ 2011/the-art-and-craft-of-the-async-snippet/*. Originally published on Dec 04, 2011.

CHAPTER 5

Carrier Networks: Down the Rabbit Hole

Tim Kadlec

There's a point in Lewis Carroll's *Alice's Adventures in Wonderland* where Alice believes she may never be able to leave the room she has found herself in after following the rabbit down its hole. She starts to question her decision:

> I almost wish I hadn't gone down that rabbit hole—and yet—and yet—it's rather curious, you know, this kind of life.

The world of mobile performance can feel the same—particularly when you start to explore mobile carrier networks. If you're looking for consistency and stability, you should look elsewhere. If, on the other hand, you enjoy the energy and excitement found in the chaos that surrounds an unstable environment, then you'll find yourself right at home.

Variability

The complexity of a system may be determined by the number of its variables, and carrier networks have a lot of variables. Their performance varies dramatically depending on factors such as location, the number of people using a network, the weather, the carrier—there isn't much that you can rely on to remain static.

One study (*http://www.pcworld.com/article/167391/a_day_in_the_life_of_3g.html*) demonstrated just how much variance there can be from location to location. The test involved checking bandwidth on 3G networks for three different mobile carriers—Sprint, Verizon, and AT&T—in various cities across the United States. The diversity of the results were stunning.

The highest recorded bandwidth was 1425 kbps in New Orleans on a Verizon network. The lowest was 477 kbps in New York City in AT&T—a difference of 948 kbps. Even within a single carrier, the variation was remarkable. While Verizon topped out at 1425 kbps, their lowest recorded bandwidth was 622 kbps in Portland, Oregon.

Another informal experiment (*http://www.webperformancetoday.com/2011/10/26/in teresting-findings-3g-mobile-performance-is-up-to-10x-slower-than-throttled-broad band-service/*) was recently conducted by Joshua Bixby. Joshua randomly recorded the amounts of bandwidth and latency on his 3G network. Even within a single location, his house, the latency varied from just over 100 ms all the way up to 350 ms.

Latency

Remarkably little information about mobile network latency has been published. In 2010, Yahoo! released some information based on a small study (*http://www.yuiblog .com/blog/2010/04/08/analyzing-bandwidth-and-latency/*) they had done. Traffic coming into the YUI blog was monitored for both bandwidth and latency. These numbers were averaged by connection type and the results published as a graph. Their study showed that the average latency for a mobile connection was 430 ms, compared to only 130 ms for an average cable connection.

The study isn't foolproof. The sample size was small and the type of audience that would be visiting the YUI blog is not exactly a representation of the average person. At least it was publicly released data. Most of the rest of the latency numbers released so far come without much context; there usually isn't any mention of how it was measured.

Transcoding

Another concern with mobile networks are frequent issues caused by carrier transcoding. Many networks, for example, attempt to reduce the file size of images. Sometimes, this is done without being noticed. Often, however, the result is that images become grainy or blurry and the appearance of the site is affected in a negative way.

The *Financial Times* worked to avoid this issue with their mobile web app by using dataURIs instead (*http://www.tomhume.org/2011/10/appftcom-and-the-cost-of-cross -platform-web-apps.html*), but even this technique is not entirely safe. While the issue is not well documented or isolated yet, a few developers in the UK have reported that O2, one of the largest mobile providers in the UK, will sometimes strip out dataURIs.

Transcoding doesn't stop at images. T-Mobile was recently found to be stripping out anything that looked like a Javascript comment (*http://www.mysociety.org/2011/08/11/ mobile-operators-breaking-content/*). The intentions were mostly honorable, but the method leads to issues. The jQuery library, for example, has a string that contains */ *. Later on in the library, you can again find the same string. Seeing these two strings, T-Mobile would then strip out everything that was in between—breaking many sites in the process.

This method of transcoding could also create issues for anyone who is trying to lazy-load their Javascript by first commenting it out (*http://googlecode.blogspot.com/2009/ 09/gmail-for-mobile-html5-series-reducing.html*) — a popular and effective technique for improving parse and page load time.

One carrier, Optus, not only causes blurry images by lowering the image resolution, but also injects an external script into the page in a blocking manner (*http://www.zdnet .com.au/optus-3g-accelerator-spawns-blurry-pics-339303393.htm*). Unfortunately, most of these transcoding issues and techniques are not very exposed or well documented. I suspect countless others are just waiting to be discovered.

Gold in Them There Hills

This can all sound a bit discouraging, but that's not the goal here. We need to explore carrier networks further because there is an incredible wealth of information we can unearth if we're willing to dig far enough.

One example of this is the idea of inactivity timers and state machines that Steve Souders was recently testing (*http://www.stevesouders.com/blog/2011/09/21/making-a-mobile -connection/*). Mobile networks rely on different states to determine allotted throughput, which in turn affects battery drain. To down-switch between states (thereby reducing battery drain, but also throughput) the carrier sends an inactivity timer. The inactivity timer signals to the device that it should shift to a more energy-efficient state. This can have a large impact on performance because it can take a second or two to ramp back up to the highest state. This inactivity timer, as you might suspect, varies from carrier to carrier. Steve has set up a test (*http://stevesouders.com/ms/*) that you can run in an attempt to identify where the inactivity timer might fire on your current connection. The results, while not foolproof, do strongly suggest that these timers can be dramatically different.

We need more of this kind of information and testing. Networks weren't originally optimized for data; they were optimized for voice. When 3G networks were rolled out, the expectation was that the major source of data traffic would come from things like picture messaging. The only accessible mobile Internet was WAP—a very simplified version of the Web.

As devices became more and more capable, however, it became possible to experience the full Internet on these devices. People started expecting to see not just a limited version of the Internet, but the whole thing (videos, cat pictures, and all) leaving the networks overwhelmed.

There are undoubtedly other techniques, similar to these transcoding methods and state machines, that carriers are doing to get around the limitations of their network in order to provide faster data services to more customers.

4G Won't Save Us

Many people like to point to the upcoming roll-out of 4G networks as a way of alleviating many of these concerns. To some extent, they're right—it will indeed help with some of the latency and bandwidth issues. However, it's a pretty costly endeavor for carriers to make that switch meaning that we shouldn't expect widespread roll-out overnight.

Even when the switch has been made we can expect that the quality, coverage and methods of optimization used by the carriers will not be uniform. William Gibson said, "The future is already here—it's just not evenly distributed." Something very similar could be said of mobile connectivity.

Where Do We Go from Here?

To move this discussion forward, we need a few things. For starters, some improved communication between developers, manufacturers, and carriers would go a long, long way. If not for AT&T's research paper (*http://www.research.att.com/articles/featured _stories/2011_03/201102_Energy_efficient*), we may still not be aware of the performance impact of carrier state machines and inactivity timers. More information like this not only cues us into the unique considerations of optimizing for mobile performance, but also gives us a bit of perspective. We are reminded that it's not just about load time; there are other factors at play and we need to consider the trade-offs.

Improved communication could also go a long way toward reducing the issues caused by transcoding methods. Take the case of T-Mobile's erroneous comment stripping. Had there been some sort of open dialogue with developers before implementing this method, the issues would probably have been caught well before the feature made it live.

We could also use a few more tools. The number—and quality—of mobile performance testing tools is improving. Yet we still have precious few tools at our disposal for testing performance on real devices, over real networks. As the Navigation Timing API (*https: //dvcs.w3.org/hg/webperf/raw-file/tip/specs/NavigationTiming/Overview.html*)   gains adoption, that will help to improve the situation. However, there will still be ample room for the creation of more robust testing tools as well.

Light at the End of the Tunnel

You know, eventually Alice gets out of that little room. She goes on to have many adventures and meet many interesting creatures. After she wakes up, she thinks what a wonderful dream it had been. As our tools continue to improve and we explore this rabbit hole further, one day we, too, will be able to make some sense of all of this. When we do our applications and our sites will be better for it.

To comment on this chapter, please visit *http://calendar.perfplanet.com/2011/carrier-networks-down-the-rabbit-hole/*. Originally published on Dec 05, 2011.

CHAPTER 6

The Need for Parallelism in HTTP

Brian Pane

Introduction: Falling Down the Stairs

The image on Figure 6-1 is part of a waterfall diagram showing the HTTP requests that an IE8 browser performed to download the graphics on the home page of an e-commerce website.

 The site name and URLs are blurred to conceal the site's identity. It would be unfair to single out one site by name as an example of poor performance when, as we'll see later, so many others suffer the same problem.

The stair-step pattern seen in this waterfall sample shows several noteworthy things:

- The client used six concurrent, persistent connections per server hostname, a typical (*http://www.browserscope.org/?category=network*) configuration among modern desktop browsers.

- On each of these connections, *the browser issued HTTP requests serially*: it waited for a response to each request before sending the next request.

- All the requests in this sequence were independent of each other; the image URLs were specified in a CSS file loaded earlier in the waterfall. Thus, significantly, *it would be valid for a client to download all these images in parallel*.

- The round-trip time (RTT) between the client and server was approximately 125ms. Thus many of these requests for small objects took just over 1 RTT. The elapsed time the browser spent downloading all N of the small images on the page was very close to (N * RTT / 6), demonstrating that the download time was largely a function of the number of HTTP requests (divided by six, thanks to the browser's use of multiple connections).

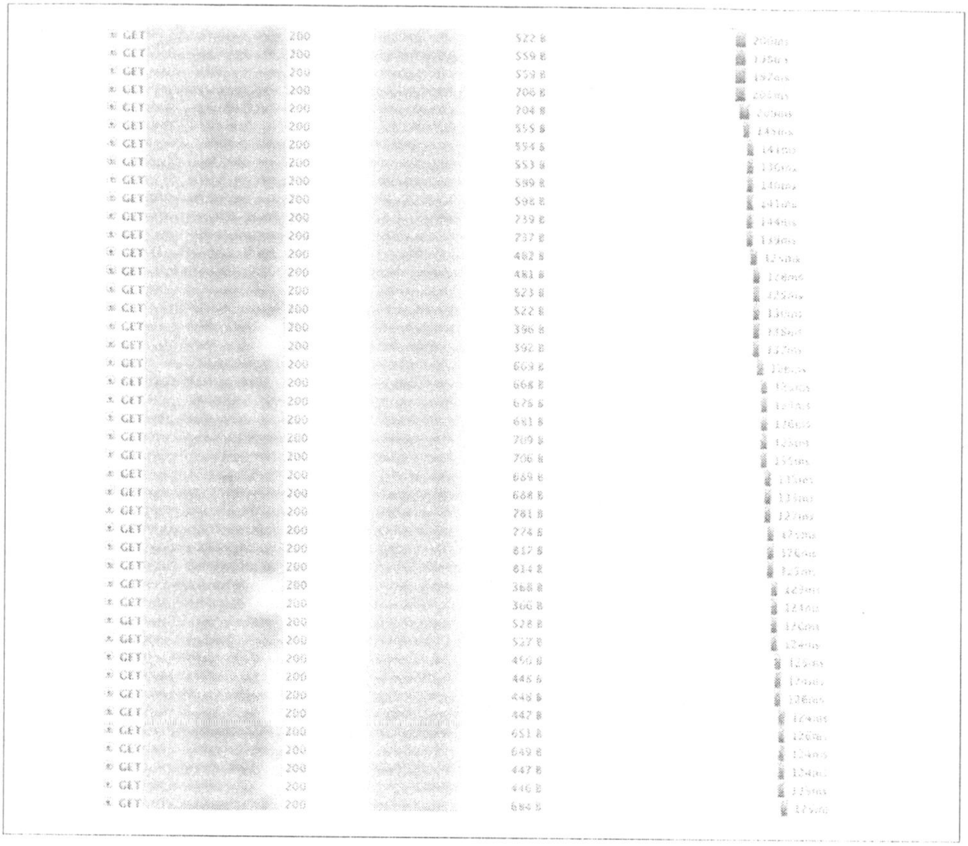

Figure 6-1. Stair-step waterfall pattern

- The amount of response data was quite small: a total of 25KB in about 1 second during this part of the waterfall, for an average throughput of under 0.25 Mb/s. The client in this test run had several Mb/s of downstream network bandwidth, so *the serialization of requests resulted in inefficient utilization of the available bandwidth.*

Current Best Practices: Working around HTTP

There are several well-established techniques for avoiding this stair-step pattern and its (N * RTT / 6) elapsed time. Besides using CDNs to reduce the RTT and client-side caching to reduce the effective value of N, the website developer can apply several *content optimizations*:

- Sprite the images.
- Inline the images as data: URIs in a stylesheet.

- If some of the images happen to be gradients or rounded corners, use CSS3 features to eliminate the need for those images altogether.
- Apply domain sharding to increase the denominator of (N * RTT / 6) by a small constant factor.

Although these content optimizations are well known, examples like the waterfall in Figure 6-1 show that they are not always applied. In the author's experience, even performance-conscious organizations sometimes launch slow websites, because speed is just one of many priorities competing for limited development time.

Thus an interesting question is: how well has the average website avoided the stair-step HTTP request serialization pattern?

Experiment: Mining the HTTP Archive

The HTTP Archive (*http://httparchive.org/*) is a database containing detailed records of the HTTP requests–including timing data with 1ms resolution that a real browser is-sued when downloading the home pages of tens of thousands of websites from the Alexa worldwide top sites list.

With this data set, we can find serialized sequences of requests in each web page. The first step is to download each page's HAR (*http://www.softwareishard.com/blog/har-12 -spec/*) file from the HTTP Archive. This file contains a list of the HTTP requests for the page, and we can find serialized sequences of requests based on a simple, heuristic definition:

- All the HTTP requests in the serialized sequence must be GETs for the same scheme:host:port.
- Each HTTP transaction except the first must begin immediately upon the completion of some other transaction in the sequence (within the 1ms resolution of the available timing data).
- Each transaction except the last must have an HTTP response status of 2xx.
- Each transaction except the last must have a response content-type of `image/png`, `image/gif`, or `image/jpeg`.

This definition captures the concept of a set of HTTP requests that are run sequentially because the browser lacks a way to run them in parallel, rather than because of content interdependencies among the requested resources. The definition errs on the side of caution by excluding non-image requests, on the grounds that a JavaScript, CSS, or SWF file might be a prerequisite for any request that follows. In the discussion that follows, we err slightly on the side of optimism by assuming that the browser knew the URLs of all the images in a serialized sequence at the beginning of the sequence.

Results: Serialization Abounds

The histogram on Figure 6-2 shows the distribution of the longest serialized request sequences per page among 49,854 web pages from the HTTP Archive's December 1, 2011 data set.

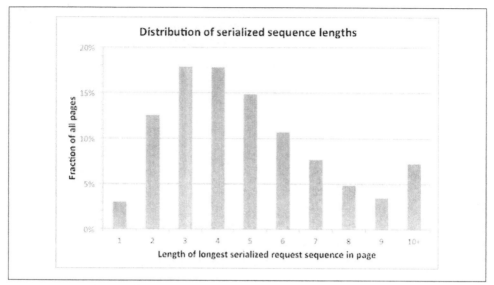

Figure 6-2. Distribution of the longest serialized request sequences per page

In approximately 3% of the web pages in this survey, there is no serialization of requests (i.e., the longest serialized request length is one). From a request parallelization perspective, these pages already are quite well optimized.

In the next 30% of the web pages, the longest serialized request sequence has a length of two or three. These pages might benefit modestly from increased request parallelization, and a simple approach like domain sharding would suffice.

The remaining two thirds of the web pages have serialized request sequences of length 4 or greater. While content optimizations could improve the request parallelization of these pages, the fact that so many sites have so much serialization suggests that the barriers to content optimization are nontrivial.

Recommendations: Time to Fix the Protocols

One way to speed up websites without content optimization would be through more widespread implementation of HTTP request pipelining. HTTP/1.1 has supported pipelining since RFC 2068, but most desktop browsers have not implemented the feature due to concerns about broken proxies that mishandle pipelined requests. In addition, head-of-queue blocking is a nontrivial problem; recent efforts have focused on ways for the server to give the clients hints (*http://tools.ietf.org/html/draft-notting ham-http-pipeline-01*) about what resources are safe to pipeline. Mobile browsers, however, are beginning to use pipelining more commonly.

Another approach is to introduce a multiplexing session layer beneath HTTP, so that the client can issue requests in parallel. An example of this strategy is SPDY (*http://www .chromium.org/spdy*), supported currently in Chrome and soon (*http://bitsup.blogspot .com/2011/11/video-of-spdy-talk-at-codebitseu.html*) in Firefox.

Whether through pipelining or multiplexing, it appears worthwhile for the industry to pursue protocol-level solutions to increase HTTP request parallelization.

 To comment on this chapter, please visit *http://calendar.perfplanet.com/ 2011/the-need-for-parallelism-in-http/*. Originally published on Dec 06, 2011.

CHAPTER 7

Automating Website Performance

Josh Fraser

I believe that automation is the next phase for web performance optimization. There are a lot of optimizations that are tedious to implement by hand or can simply be done better in an automated fashion. Of course, this is exactly what we're doing at Torbit (*http://torbit.com/*) — taking all the best practices and making the benefits accessible to everyone without you having to worry about the technical details.

Here, I present some of the challenges of automation and some of the lessons we have learned from optimizing hundreds of sites with our service. I explain why it is dangerous to go down the list of YSlow (*http://developer.yahoo.com/performance/rules.html*) or Page Speed (*http://code.google.com/speed/page-speed/docs/rules_intro.html*) optimizations and attempt to automate them without thinking through the broader implications.

In the early days of Torbit, we built a filter that minified and combined CSS files. Pretty simple, right? What could go possibly go wrong? To our surprise, this "safe" filter broke a surprising number of sites. After investigating, we discovered that many sites have invalid or broken CSS that had gone unnoticed by the site owners. To understand how this happens, you need to consider how browsers handle CSS errors. Most browsers will stop parsing a CSS file as soon as they run into a syntax error. When you blindly combine CSS, those errors that used to be at the bottom of a file (and therefore didn't matter) are now in the middle of one big file. What may have been a small issue that didn't affect anything, could now be breaking the entire layout of the site.

The obvious solution was to fix or remove the offending CSS rule and that was exactly what we did. We "fixed" their broken CSS files first and then combined them. Unfortunately, fixing their CSS had unintended consequences. We hadn't considered the fact that developers had been hacking around their broken CSS. In fact, in some cases these bugs had become so baked into their websites that removing them often completely destroyed the visual look of the site. What are you supposed to do when fixing someones code totally breaks their site?

Ultimately, we built a Smart CSS Loader (*http://torbit.com/blog/2011/11/17/a-better-way-to-load-css/*), which allows us to download all of the CSS files for a web page in one request, while still applying each of the files to the DOM individually. This method not only solves the issues from broken CSS, but includes other benefits like being non-blocking and taking advantage of HTML5 localStorage whenever possible.

The lesson here is to follow the principles, but not necessarily the specific rules. In the CSS example, the underlying principle was to reduce HTTP requests, and this goal holds true whether you are doing the optimizations by hand or in an automated fashion. The specific rule of combining CSS files obviously needed some rethinking in order to be able to apply that optimization to any site without breaking anything.

One of the benefits of going back to the fundamentals is that it opens your mind to find other performance optimizations you would have missed if you had simply focused on the YSlow or Page Speed rules. Some of the best optimizations we have at Torbit aren't mentioned by either YSlow or Page Speed. For example, converting images to WebP format (*http://torbit.com/blog/2011/04/05/torbit-adds-support-for-webp/*) and serving them for targeted browsers is a great optimization that can significantly minimize payload, but it isn't on the list. Using localStorage to cut down on HTTP requests and improve caching (*http://torbit.com/blog/2011/05/31/localstorage-mobile-performance/*) is also not mentioned. To be fair, those tools are primarily for developers and optimizations like these don't make sense for most businesses to implement by hand. The fact that these optimizations are neither easy nor fun to do by hand is what makes them such perfect candidates for automation.

If you want to automate, it's important to focus on the basics. Remember the principles. Make things smaller, move them closer, cache them longer, and load them more intelligently. Focus on the end objective and don't get too caught up in the rules.

 To comment on this chapter, please visit *http://calendar.perfplanet.com/2011/automating-website-performance/*. Originally published on Dec 07, 2011.

CHAPTER 8

Frontend SPOF in Beijing

Steve Souders

I'm at Velocity China in Beijing as I write this article for the Performance Calendar. Since this is my second time to Beijing I was better prepared for the challenges of being behind the Great Firewall. I knew I couldn't access popular U.S. websites like Google, Facebook, and Twitter, but as I did my typical surfing I was surprised at how many other websites seemed to be blocked.

Business Insider

It didn't take me long to realize the problem was frontend SPOF (*http://www.stevesoud ers.com/blog/2010/06/01/frontend-spof/*)—when a frontend resource (script, stylesheet, or font file) causes a page to be unusable. Some pages were completely blank, such as Business Insider (*http://www.businessinsider.com*, Figure 8-1).

Firebug's Net Panel shows that `anywhere.js` is taking a long time to download because it's coming from `platform.twitter.com` – which is blocked by the firewall. Knowing that scripts block rendering of all subsequent DOM elements, we form the hypothesis that `anywhere.js` is being loaded in blocking mode in the HEAD. Looking at the HTML source, we see that's exactly what is happening:

```
<head>
...
<!-- Twitter Anywhere -->
<script src="https://platform.twitter.com/anywhere.js?id=ZVO...&v=1"
        type="text/javascript"></script>
<!-- / Twitter Anywhere -->
...

</head>

<body>
```

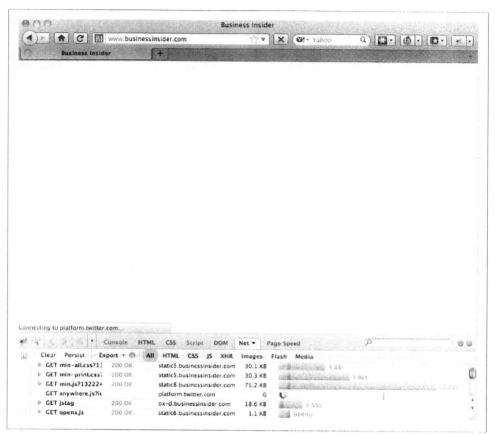

Figure 8-1. The dreaded "blank white screen" due to a blocking Twitter script

If `anywhere.js` had been loaded asynchronously (*http://www.stevesouders.com/blog/ 2009/04/27/loading-scripts-without-blocking/*) this wouldn't happen. Instead, since `any where.js` is loaded the old way with `<SCRIPT SRC=...`, it blocks all the DOM elements that follow which in this case is the entire BODY of the page. If we wait long enough the request for `anywhere.js` times out and the page begins to render. How long does it take for the request to timeout? Looking at the "after" screenshot of Business Insider we see it takes *1 minute and 15 seconds* for the request to timeout. That's 1 minute and 15 seconds that the user is left staring at a blank white screen waiting for the Twitter script! (See Figure 8-2.)

CNET

CNET (*http://www.cnet.com/*) has a slightly different experience; the navigation header is displayed but the rest of the page is blocked from rendering (Figure 8-3).

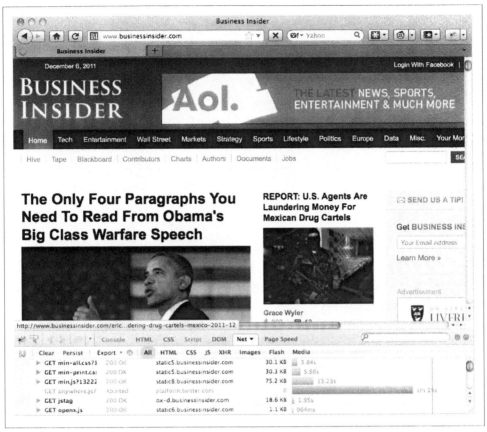

Figure 8-2. Business Insider finally renders after 1 minute 15 seconds

Looking in Firebug we see that `wrapper.js` from `cdn.eyewonder.com` is "pending"—this must be another domain that's blocked by the firewall. Based on where the rendering stops, our guess is that the `wrapper.js` SCRIPT tag is immediately after the navigation header and is loaded in blocking mode thus preventing the rest of the page from rendering. The HTML confirms that this is indeed what's happening:

```
<header>
...
</header>

<script src="http://cdn.eyewonder.com/100125/771933/1592365/wrapper.js"></script>

<div id="rb_wrap">

<div id="rb_content"> <div id="contentMain">
```

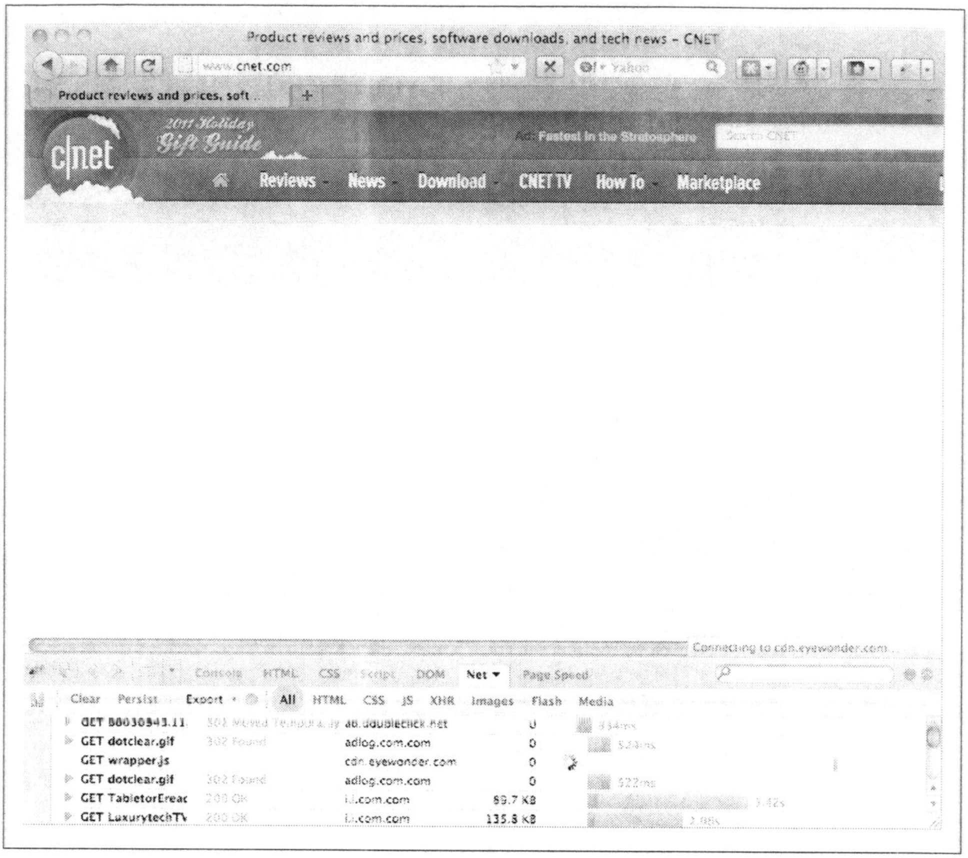

Figure 8-3. CNET rendering is blocked by ads from eyewonder.com

O'Reilly Radar

Everyday, I visit O'Reilly Radar to read Nat Torkington's (*http://radar.oreilly.com/nat/index.html*) Four Short Links. Normally Nat's is one of many stories on the Radar front page, but going there from Beijing shows a page with only one story (Figure 8-4).

At the bottom of this first story there's supposed to be a Tweet button. This button is added by the `widgets.js` script fetched from `platform.twitter.com` which is blocked by the Great Firewall. This wouldn't be an issue if `widgets.js` was fetched asynchronously, but sadly a peek at the HTML shows that's not the case:

```
<a href="...">Comment</a>
 | 
<span class="social-counters">
<span class="retweet">
<a href="http://twitter.com/share" class="twitter-share-button"
   data-count="horizontal"
```

```
    data-url="http://radar.oreilly.com/2011/12/four-short-links-6-december-20-1.html"
    data-text="Four short links: 6 December 2011" data-via="radar"
    data-related="oreillymedia:oreilly.com">Tweet</a>
<script src="http://platform.twitter.com/widgets.js"
    type="text/javascript"></script>
</span>
```

Figure 8-4. O'Reilly Radar rendering is blocked by Twitter widget.

The Cause of Frontend SPOF

One possible takeaway from these examples might be that frontend SPOF is specific to Twitter and eyewonder and a few other third-party widgets. Sadly, frontend SPOF can be caused by any third-party widget, and even from the main website's own scripts, stylesheets, or font files.

Another possible takeaway from these examples might be to avoid third-party widgets that are blocked by the Great Firewall. But the Great Firewall isn't the only cause of frontend SPOF—it just makes it easier to reproduce. Any script, stylesheet, or font file that takes a long time to return has the potential to cause frontend SPOF. This typically happens when there's an outage or some other type of failure, such as an overloaded server where the HTTP request languishes in the server's queue for so long the browser times out.

The true cause of frontend SPOF is loading a script, stylesheet, or font file in a blocking manner. The table in my frontend SPOF (*http://www.stevesouders.com/blog/2010/06/01/frontend-spof/*) blog post shows when this happens. It's really the website owner who controls whether or not their site is vulnerable to frontend SPOF. So what's a website owner to do?

Avoiding Frontend SPOF

The best way to avoid frontend SPOF is to load scripts asynchronously. Many popular third-party widgets do this by default, such as Google Analytics (*http://code.google.com/apis/analytics/docs/tracking/asyncTracking.html*), Facebook (*https://developers.facebook.com/docs/reference/plugins/like/*), and Meebo (*http://blog.meebo.com/?p=2956*). Twitter also has an async snippet (*https://dev.twitter.com/docs/tweet-button*) for the Tweet button that O'Reilly Radar should use. If the widgets you use don't offer an async version you can try Stoyan's Social button BFFs (*http://www.phpied.com/social-button-bffs/*) async pattern.

Another solution is to wrap your widgets in an iframe. This isn't always possible, but in two of the examples above the widget is eventually served in an iframe. Putting them in an iframe from the start would have avoided the frontend SPOF problems.

For the sake of brevity I've focused on solutions for scripts. Solutions for font files can be found in my @font-face and performance (*http://www.stevesouders.com/blog/2009/10/13/font-face-and-performance/*) blog post. I'm not aware of much research on loading stylesheets asynchronously. Causing too many reflows and FOUC (*http://bluerobot.com/web/css/fouc.asp/*) are concerns that need to be addressed.

Call to Action

Business Insider, CNET, and O'Reilly Radar all have visitors from China, and yet the way their pages are constructed delivers a bad user experience where most if not all of the page is blocked for more than a minute. This isn't a P2 frontend JavaScript issue. *This is an outage.* If the backend servers for these websites took 1 minute to send back a response, you can bet the DevOps teams at Business Insider, CNET, and O'Reilly wouldn't sleep until the problem was fixed. So why is there so little concern about frontend SPOF?

Frontend SPOF doesn't get much attention—it definitely doesn't get the attention it deserves given how easily it can bring down a website. One reason is it's hard to diagnose. There are a lot of monitors that will start going off if a server response time exceeds

60 seconds. And since all that activity is on the backend it's easier to isolate the cause. Is it that pagers don't go off when clientside page load times exceed 60 seconds? That's hard to believe, but perhaps that's the case.

Perhaps it's the way page load times are tracked. If you're looking at worldwide medians, or even averages, and China isn't a major audience, your page load time stats might not exceed alert levels when frontend SPOF happens. Or maybe page load times are mostly tracked using synthetic testing, and those user agents aren't subjected to real world issues like the Great Firewall.

One thing website owners can do is ignore frontend SPOF until it's triggered by some future outage. A quick calculation shows this is a scary choice. If a third-party widget has a 99.99% uptime and a website has five widgets that aren't async, the probability of frontend SPOF is 0.05%. If we drop uptime to 99.9%, the probability of frontend SPOF climbs to 0.5%. Five widgets might be high, but remember that "third-party widget" includes ads and metrics. Also, the website's own resources can cause frontend SPOF which brings the number even higher. The average website today contains 14 scripts (*http://httparchive.org/trends.php#bytesJS&reqJS*) any of which could cause frontend SPOF if they're not loaded async.

Frontend SPOF is a real problem that needs more attention. Website owners should use async snippets and patterns, monitor real user page load times, and look beyond averages to 95th percentiles and standard deviations. Doing these things will mitigate the risk of subjecting users to the dreaded blank white page. A chain is only as strong as its weakest link. What's your website's weakest link? There's a lot of focus on backend resiliency. I'll wager your weakest link is on the frontend.

 To comment on this chapter, please visit *http://calendar.perfplanet.com/ 2011/frontend-spof-in-beijing/*. Originally published on Dec 08, 2011.

CHAPTER 9

All about YSlow

Betty Tso

Since 2007, millions of developers have been using YSlow to help them find out ways to make their web pages load faster. YSlow score has been the standard for Performance measurement in dev, QA, and production stages.

YSlow first started as a bookmarklet by Steve Souders while at Yahoo!, and soon became a popular Firefox extension. Over the past year, Marcel Duran built a YSlow Chrome extension, Opera extension, and Safari extension. In order to also support mobile devices as well as other browsers, YSlow was also made available as a bookmarklet in June 2011 with fresh shiny code and new architecture.

While speaking at Velocity China (*http://velocity.oreilly.com.cn/2011/*) on December 7, 2011, our team announced the release of YSlow for Command Line beta (*https://github .com/marcelduran/yslow/wiki/Command-Line-(HAR)*), with courtesy to our FE tech lead, Marcel. This version leverages Node.js and takes *.har* files as input to generate YSlow score for a URL. Several output options are available—JSON, XML, and plain text. Users can also pipe the result to a beacon server, such as `http://www.showslow.com/beacon/yslow/` and view the result in a graphical UI. For complete YSlow beacon spec, refer to the users' guide (*https://github.com/marcelduran/yslow/wiki/User-Guide#wiki -yslow_beacon*).

In February 2012, YSlow was open sourced on Github and given a new home: yslow.org (*http://yslow.org*). Since then, YSlow has become a community-driven tool —within the first 24 hours of the open source announcement, there were 437 watchers and 37 forks.

While speaking at Amazon's annual frontend conference in April 2012 (*wh.yslow.org/ amazon-wdc*), Marcel Duran announced YSlow for PhantomJS (*https://github.com/mar celduran/yslow/wiki/PhantomJS*), a command-line script that allows page performance analysis from live URLs.

The diagram in Figure 9-1 captures the timeline of YSlow development over the past few years as of December 9, 2011.

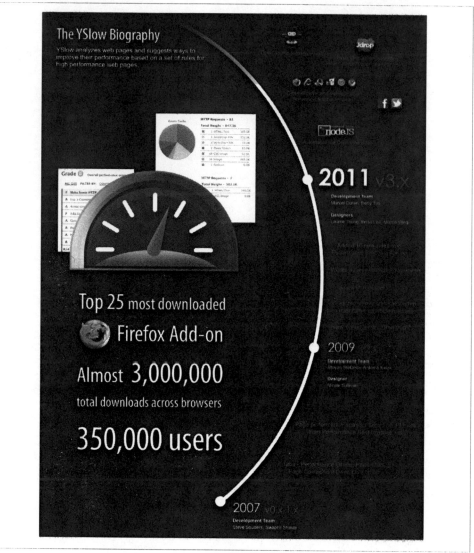

Figure 9-1. YSlow timeline

Did you know...?

- YSlow can also be used as a framework to build extensions that talk to browsers. Refer to Stoyan Stefanov's article for code samples: Web Testing Framework (*http://www.phpied.com/wtf/*).

- Starting from v3.0.5, YSlow has a new feature: one-click-add-cdn to CDN custom list, which allows user to add CDNs to a custom list when applicable.

- YSlow's social feature lets users share their YSlow score with Facebook and Twitter friends; the link shared points to YSlow Scoremeter on getyslow.com (*http://yslow .org/scoremeter/*). With the Scoremeter, the user is able to estimate the impact of a fix on the resulted YSlow score. Here is a sample link shared on my Facebook: example Scoremeter (*http://yhoo.it/KNWv5k*).
- Here is the full list of YSlow backlog features (*http://wh.yslow.org/yslow-backlog*).

As always, we would love to hear your feedback. You can reach us on the official site (*http://yslow.org*), Facebook (*http://www.facebook.com/getyslow*), Twitter (*http://www .twitter.com/getyslow*), or via email at ask@yslow.org.

Special thanks to Lauren Tsung, who created the infographic in this post. Lauren is currently working as an interactive designer in Yahoo! System Tools team.

 To comment on this chapter, please visit *http://calendar.perfplanet.com/ 2011/all-aboout-yslow/*. Originally published on Dec 09, 2011.

CHAPTER 10

Secrets of High Performance Native Mobile Applications

Israel Nir

Since Steve Souders published his seminal book *High Performance Web Sites* four years ago, the world has changed considerably. Web sites became faster, browsers significantly improved and users started to expect top performance. During these four years, a new category of client-facing applications was born, which currently receives little attention from the performance community—native mobile applications. These applications have their own set of challenges and opportunities. Luckily, they also have a lot in common with good old web applications. One thing's for certain, users expect native apps to perform as fast, if not faster, than web sites. With the Christmas rush in full swing, users are bound to be even less tolerant of poorly performing apps, so I figured it's a good time to see how the top sellers' mobile apps perform, and at the same time, also make a dent in my holiday gift list.

What are the two factors that most affect app performance? I'm not going to discuss native code tweaks, since this is predominantly platform-dependent and will probably put most of you to sleep. So let's focus on mobile performance tuning—improving the application's behavior over the network. The importance of network utilization is even greater considering the kind of network conditions these apps are most likely to encounter, such as high latency and low bandwidth.

In order to analyze a mobile app's network traffic, you can start by setting up an ad-hoc WiFi network on a computer, connect your mobile device to that network and run a packet capture on the computer. Then use an application such as Wireshark to examine the traffic generated by your application, or load the packet capture into a tool like PcapPerf. Another option is to use a proxy, such as Charles Proxy of Fiddler, but please be aware that it may impact your app's network behavior, such as limiting the number of concurrent connections. Personally I use my company's tools (Shunra vCat with Analytics, *http://www.shunra.com/products/shunra-vcat*) to capture and analyze the app's traffic. These tools also enable me to emulate mobile networks, so it's easier for me to detect problems that may only manifest on various mobile networks, such as 3G.

Keep an Eye on Your Waterfalls

Time to start some serious shopping, so let's look at one of the major mobile retail players. Starting with Mom, the world traveller, I thought a new luggage set would be appreciated. Lots of choices here—now what's her favorite color? I had lots of time to ponder this question, because this retailer's iPhone app takes quite a while to load. Examination of the HTTP waterfall reveals a long daisy chain of resources blocking each other, lasting for 7.5 seconds. Notice that in this case, images are blocking parallel downloads, which is something you won't typically see in a web app (Figure 10-1).

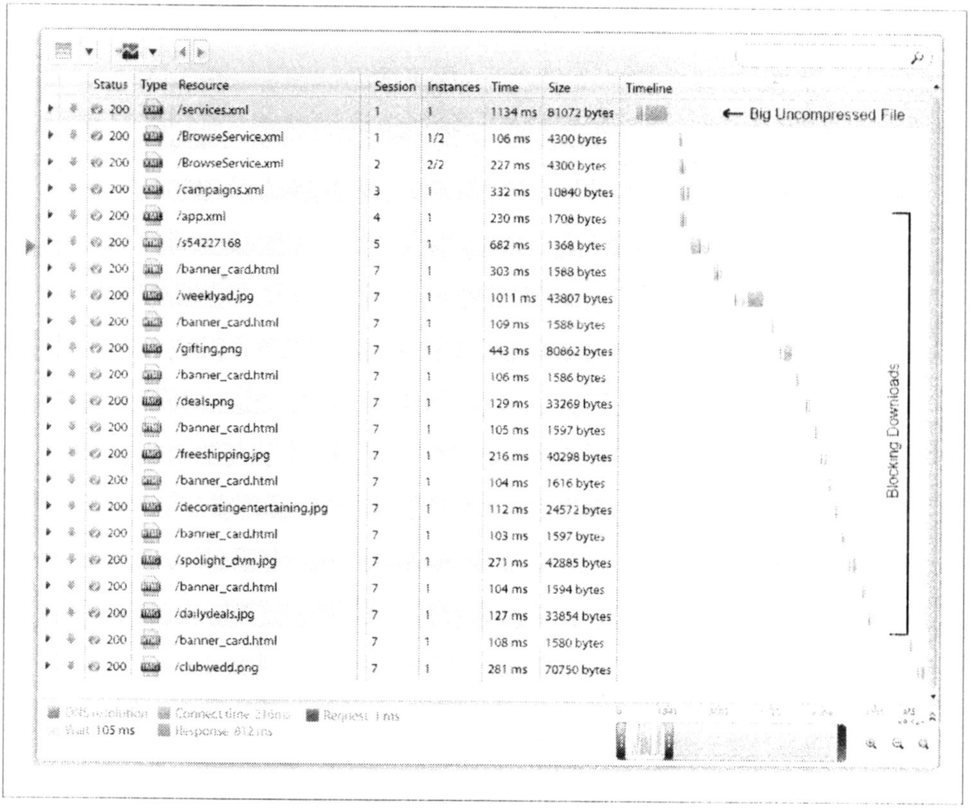

Figure 10-1. Blocking downloads

While web developers can enable parallel downloads with a few simple tweaks and put their trust in browser makers, it's up to the native app developer to come up with the optimal concurrent download scheme. Our research shows that even on mobile net-

---

works you can obtain a performance gain by using up to four parallel downloads, and advanced users can switch to HTTP pipelining to acquire another speed boost.

Compress Those Resources

In the waterfall in Figure 10-1, you may notice that the first resource, *services.xml* is 81KB long and takes more than a second to fetch over the network (blocking any other resources following it). Of that second, 812ms are spent just downloading the file. Looking at the response headers one can see that it was sent uncompressed. If it were compressed, it would have weighted only 6KB, saving at least half a second in response time. Obviously, it's not the only resource sent uncompressed using this app (Figure 10-2).

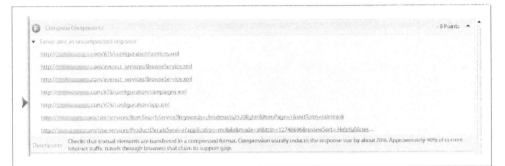

Figure 10-2. Uncompressed resources

Don't Download the Same Content Twice

This should be a no brainer, but we have observed this performance anti-pattern in so many Android and iPhone apps that it's worth pointing out. When implementing a native app, it's the developer's responsibility to implement a basic caching mechanism. Just setting the caching-headers of http responses is usually not enough. Here's what happened when I was looking for a baby gift using the iPhone app of an e-commerce site known for its handmade items (Figure 10-3).

Cute baby, but the same image was downloaded three times, and this was typical for many other images that were also downloaded multiple times. Moreover, some images downloaded more than one instance in the same TCP session. Creating a basic caching layer, one that caches elements in memory as long as the application is running, is not that complicated. It greatly improves performance and highlights your professionalism.

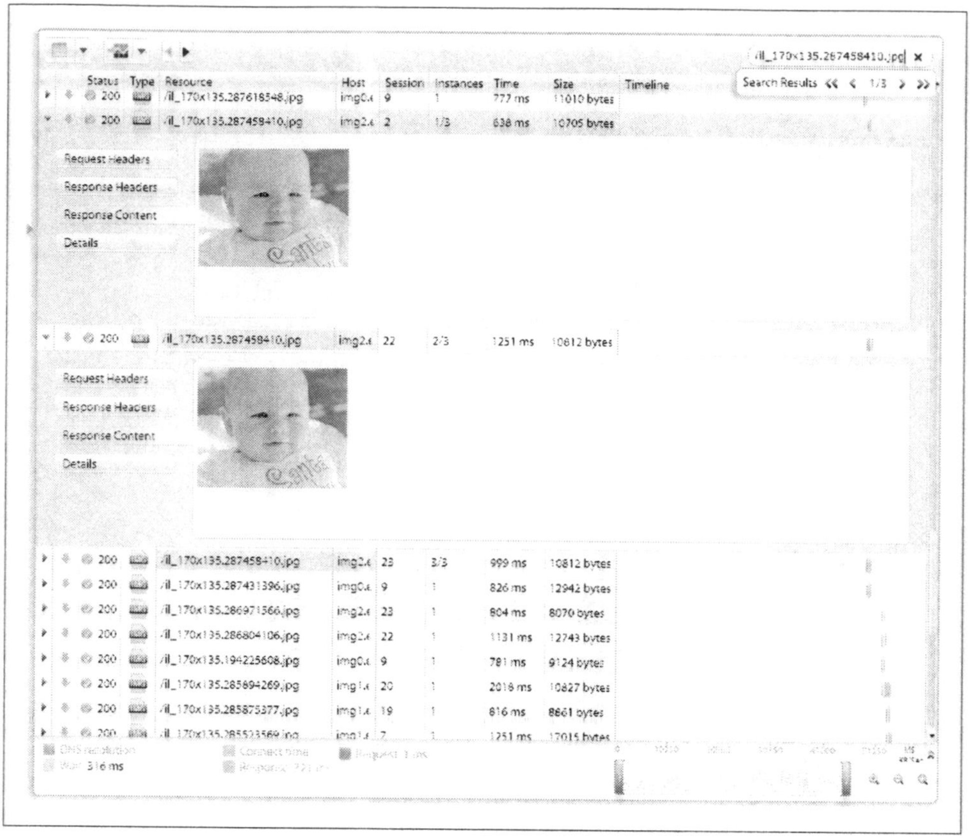

Figure 10-3. Duplicate images

Can Too Much Adriana Lima Slow You Down?

Tired of looking for the usual Christmas presents, I launched a famous lingerie retailer's app, looking for, hmmm, stockings to put in my girlfriend's Christmas stocking. Though I enjoy looking at Adriana Lima as much as the next guy, downloading huge images of her and the other VS models was actually quite painful. Surprisingly, although I was using an iPhone, I was getting both iPhone and iPad versions of the images. The iPad images were obviously not optimized for my small screen, and amounted to half a megabyte of wasted traffic. Although this might be OK over a wired network, it's exasperating on a mobile (Figure 10-4).

During the past year we have encountered many applications that exhibit similar performance faux-pas. Hipmunk, the hip flight search application, downloaded a big data file (*http://www.shunra.com/shunrablog/index.php/2011/03/21/being-slow-is-not-hip/*) (650KB after compression), containing the entire search results in one chunk. It would have been better to split that file into several smaller files, some of which could be downloaded asynchronously. Other applications download many very small files that

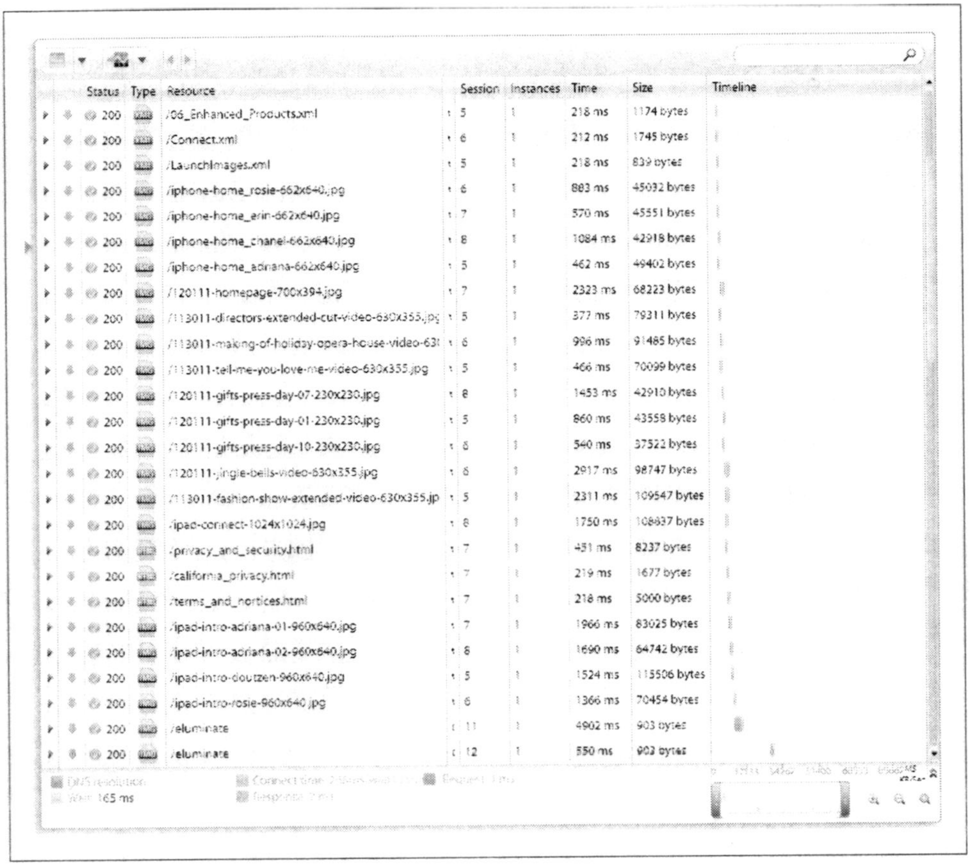

Figure 10-4. Duplicate images with iPad versions served to iPhone

could be easily combined into fewer larger files to circumvent a performance hit due to the high latency in mobile networks.

Epilogue

This is just a short sample of performance best-practices for native mobile apps, indicating that some of the principals of well-performing native apps and websites are not that different. Eliminate unnecessary downloads (with respect to both the number of bytes and the number of requests), and manage the rest to make good use of the network by leveraging parallelization and asynchronous downloads. While with web sites you relegate many of those tasks to the browser, with native apps it's mostly up to you. The room for performance tweaks is much larger, but so is the room for mistakes. Thus, if there's one important takeaway, it's to always test your apps early and never leave performance to chance.

To comment on this chapter, please visit *http://calendar.perfplanet.com/ 2011/secrets-of-high-performance-native-mobile-applications/.* Originally published on Dec 10, 2011.

CHAPTER 11

Pure CSS3 Images? Hmm, Maybe Later

Marcel Duran

Several designers while at Yahoo! requested that the original YSlow logo PSD be used in promotional materials such as t-shirts, posters, flyers, etc. in some events that occurred along this year, I had no idea where it was ever since I joined the Exceptional Performance Team (*http://developer.yahoo.com/performance/*) to take care of YSlow (*http://yslow.org/*) amongst other performance tools. In order to solve this problem I decided to rebuild it from scratch because it didn't seem so complicated, the problem was I was a speed freak, not a designer so inspired by the famous pure CSS Twitter fail whale (*http://www.subcide.com/articles/pure-css-twitter-fail-whale/*) I put my CSS muscles to work out focusing obviously on performance to provide those designers a scalable YSlow logo (*http://wh.yslow.org/css3-logo*) for their delight as well as potentially having a smaller image payload to be used on the Web.

The Challenge

It was an interesting challenge from performance perspective since the less code I used, the smaller the final image would be and the faster it would perform (rendering time). My goal was to achieve a one-size-fits all solution to be used in the wild on the Web. Besides performance, as a front end engineer, I was also interested in how CSS3 could help solve this issue (cross-browser possibly) and the limitations imposed. I use Chrome for development, so my first goal was to make it happen for that browser first before making it cross-browser compatible. It was also easy to benchmark the rendering time, which was my main point of concern when talking about CSS3 background gradients, border radius, transformation, etc.

Getting My Hands Dirty with CSS3 Cooking

Having JSFiddle (*http://jsfiddle.net/*) as my playground was really helpful because it was a trial-and-error task, plus I could keep track of versions and share so easily. Chrome

Developer Tools: Element Styles (*http://code.google.com/chrome/devtools/docs/ele-ments-styles.html#styles_edit*) also played an important role letting me test my changes on-the-fly.

My JSFiddle playground is available at *http://jsfiddle.net/marcelduran/g7KvW/6/*, where you can see the code and final image result. The CSS and HTML code (no JavaScript here) is also listed at the end of the chapter.

The three images on the *Result* tab of the fiddle are from top-down: original (250px width) image, pure CSS3 with 250px width, and pure CSS3 with 50% width. If you load the fiddle in Chrome, you're expected to get better results. JSFiddle also allows you to fork the code and apply your own changes, so be my guest.

With 21 DOM elements (22 counting the `<style>` block) and by using uneven `border-radius` for geometries, background gradients to make it shiny, rounded, and more realistic, and some transform rotations were enough to finally get the YSlow speedometer logo without the red needle. My first attempt was to use DOM element borders to achieve a pointy triangle (*http://jonrohan.me/guide/css/creating-triangles-in-css/*) which works fine but unfortunately, it did not scale due to percentage values not being allowed (*http://www.w3.org/TR/CSS2/box.html#value-def-border-width*) on `border-width`. Also background gradients do not apply to borders either, making it not shiny as in the original image. When I hit this wall, I pinged my former co-worker Thierry Koblentz (*http://twitter.com/thierrykoblentz*), and he came to the rescue. He eats CSS not only for breakfast and is always up for CSS challenges. It was impressive, he came up with a very nice solution using rotated displaced DIVs hiding the undesired parts with `overflow:hidden`, which allowed me to make it shiny through background gradient. As a plus, he also included a nice transition that smoothly animates the needle to the max value when hovering, such feature is not available in regular PNG/JPG images.

After I reached my goal for Chrome, using basically W3C specification for CSS3 and a few `-webkit-` prefixes, it was time to attack the other browsers, so I started adding other vendors prefixes like `-moz-`, `-o-`, `-ms-`, and `filter` for Internet Explorer.

Cross-Browser Results

I got very disappointed with the cross-browser results and after spending some time trying to figure out a way to fix things for all browsers without increasing the CSS code or adding more HTML elements, I gave up and played John Lennon: "Imagine there's no cross-browser issue..." I wonder how come our honorable Performance Calendar curator (*http://twitter.com/stoyanstefanov*) hasn't thought about such a song before (*http://www.youtube.com/watch?v=bPdkWJe9XH0*).

The original image (PNG24) is shown in Figure 11-1.

Figure 11-1. original YSlow logo in PNG24 format

The screenshots for the tested browsers with comments are shown in Figure 11-2 (non-IE browsers) and Figure 11-3 (different IE versions). The left column of images in those figures shows the result when using vendor-specific CSS and the right column is W3C-valid CSS3 only.

Interesting how the W3C-only versions fall back gracefully, that shows no browser is strictly following specs or that the specs are not fully defined yet by the time of this writing. Even not fully resembling the original, with some exceptions, they all look like a speedometer gauge somehow, except er, guess who?

With that pure CSS3 image working decently at least on Chrome, I was able to provide the designers what they were after and that was enough for me to start my performance benchmarking. I know one might argue it's possible to make it work better on other browsers with more DOM elements and/or more CSS selectors/rules, but that was a time-consuming task and I was working on it during my spare time, so enough with CSS and let's see what we are here for.

Benchmarking

In order to compare real image files (*http://wh.yslow.org/css3-logo-images*) versus CSS3-generated ones (*http://wh.yslow.org/css3-logo-payload*), I created a few pages containing only one image per page, either real files URL and data URI (*http://en.wikipedia.org/wiki/Data_URI_scheme*) (&ltimg src="...">) or CSS3 (HTML + CSS `<style>` block in the same page).

Payload

Hosting these pages (*http://wh.yslow.org/css3-logo-payload*) in a local Apache server, I was able to fetch them with and without compression (`Accept-Encoding: gzip,deflate`) via `curl` (*http://curl.haxx.se/*), getting the content length for the CSS3 and data URI ones and the real images URL obviously without compression. The minified with compression lengths were used as payload per page in this benchmark (Figure 11-3).

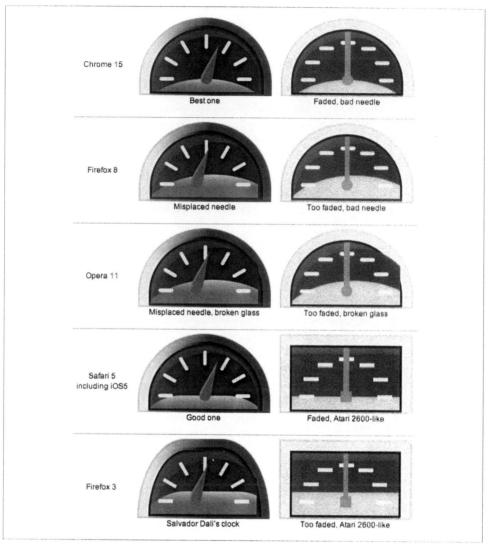

Figure 11-2. Results in non-IE browsers

Rendering

Adding a small script at the bottom of these pages (*http://wh.yslow.org/css3-logo-ren dering*) that reloads the page 100 times with 1 second interval, using `sessionStorage` (*https://developer.mozilla.org/en/DOM/Storage#sessionStorage*) for counting and with Chrome Developer Tools: Timeline Panel (*http://code.google.com/chrome/devtools/ docs/timeline.html*) recording the page activity, I was able to export the logged data (*http://wh.yslow.org/css3-logo-logs*). Then with a NodeJS script (*http://wh.yslow.org/ css3-logo-script*), I could extract and filter only the timing related to the rendering

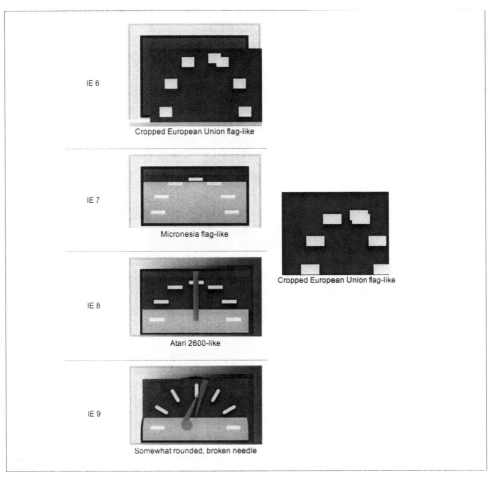

IE 6
Cropped European Union flag-like

IE 7
Micronesia flag-like

IE 8
Atari 2600-like

IE 9
Somewhat rounded, broken needle

Cropped European Union flag-like

Figure 11-3. Results in IE

activity, cleaning the top and bottom 5% of the sample to remove some noisy data, and then getting the average (*http://wh.yslow.org/css3-logo-results*) in milliseconds (Figure 11-4).

Analysis of the compared versions of YSlow logo image is shown in the table on Figure 11-5, which leads to the chart on Figure 11-6. The data for the chart is available at *http://wh.yslow.org/css3-logo-data*.

CSS3-generated images can achieve smaller payloads compared to regular images either URL or data URI ones. In this YSlow logo example, the W3C standard CSS3 is roughly 34 times smaller than PNG24 image version. Data URI versions of the same image type have around the same payload after being compressed. They get increased a few bytes only, interesting in this case that the inline version of JPG is slightly smaller than the regular JPG image file.

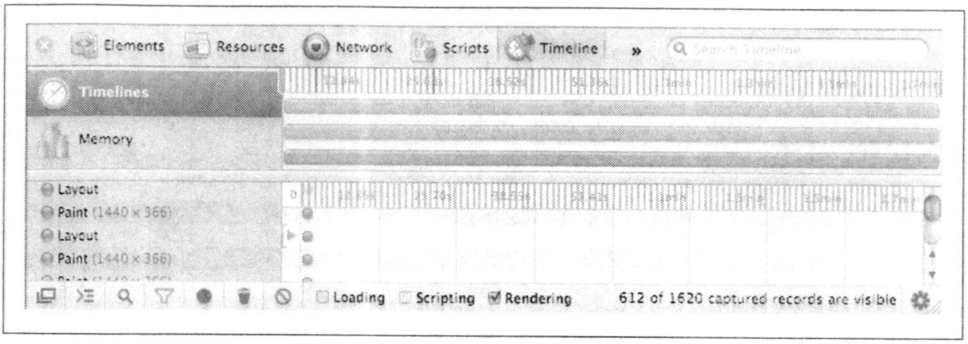

Figure 11-4. Timeline panel

On the other hand, CSS3-generated images rendering time is worse than regular images, being around 6.5 times slower than the PNG24 version. The inline versions more than double the rendering time when compared to their regular image file versions. The CSS3 W3C standard version rendering performed 2.5 times faster than `-webkit-` or the one with all browser vendors prefixes. This doesn't necessarily mean it's really faster because per the screenshots results above, none of them triggered all the CSS rules to render the logo properly according to the original version.

These rendering times were measured just by displaying the static images on the page without any hovering user interaction that animates the gauge needle on CSS3 versions. These numbers would likely to be increased in the case-scenario where users are allowed to hide-and-show or drag-and-drop images over the viewport triggering several repaint, reflow, and restyle (*http://www.phpied.com/rendering-repaint-reflowrelayout -restyle/*) on these DOM elements.

Comparing apples-to-apples quality-wise, CSS3 with all prefixes or `-webkit-` on Chrome are comparable to the PNG24 version, both have transparent background and no pixelation. CSS3 is 34 times smaller, 6.5 times slower (in order of milliseconds) and has the advantage of keeping the same payload for different sizes, while PNG would increase when resized from the original source (PSD when available) to avoid quality loss, however users are not able to save CSS3 as an image without taking screenshots.

Are We There Yet?

Not really, hopefully in the near future we'll get rid of browser vendors' specific prefixes and have a one-size-fits-all CSS solution that works equally in all browsers. But even when we get there, it's a very time-consuming task to create images from scratch, using DOM elements and styles manually (SVG is designed for this). An illustrator tool to aid drawing is in high demand for such task where one could drag over Bézier curves (*http://en.wikipedia.org/wiki/B%C3%A9zier_curve*), adjusting the control points in

Type	Pros	Cons	Payload (bytes)	Rendering (ms)
CSS3 W3C	'Standard', small	Not x-browser yet, extra markup	807	4.436
CSS3 - o-	Works on Opera	Vendor specific, extra markup	811	-
CSS3 - moz-	Works on Firefox	Vendor specific, extra markup	815	-
CSS3 - ms-	Works on IE	Vendor specific, extra markup	945	-
CSS3 - webkit-	Works on Chrome/Safari	Vendor specific, extra markup	977	11.233
CSS3 all	Covers 'all' browsers, small, animation	Unused rules, extra markup	1400	11.238
WebP	Smallest image file	Not supported by all major browsers, no transparency	4066	1.769
WebP inline	Smallest file	Non x-browser, no transparency, non IE < 8	4175	5.701
JPG inline	Smaller file, x-browser	No transparency, non IE < 8	7881	3.313
JPG	Smaller image file, x-browser	No transparency	7926	1.768
PNG8	Small image file, x-browser, transparency	Up to 256 colors	8269	1.854
PNG8 inline	Small file, transparency	Up to 256 colors, non IE < 8	8399	4.267
PNG24	High quality, alpha channel	Large image file, buggy on IE < 7	27391	1.736
PNG24 inline	High quality, alpha channel	Large file, non IE < 8	27704	5.968

Figure 11-5. The compared versions of YSlow logo image

order to get the correspondent directives to CSS3 `border-radius` shaping geometric lines properly.

 To comment on this chapter, please visit *http://calendar.perfplanet.com/ 2011/pure-css3-images-hmm-maybe-later/*. Originally published on Dec 11, 2011.

Appendix: Code Listings

You can also play with the code live at *http://jsfiddle.net/marcelduran/g7KvW/6/*.

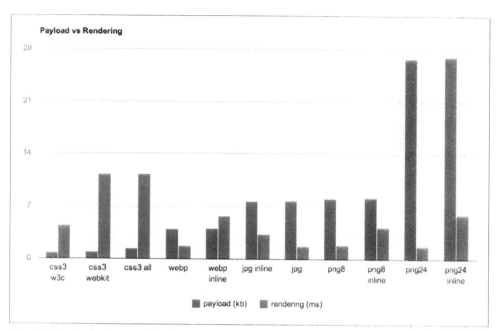

Figure 11-6. Payload versus Rendering

HTML

```
<img src="http://d.yimg.com/jc/ydn/speedometer.png">
<div class="ys" style="width:250px">
    <div class="a">
        <div class="b">
            <div class="c">
                <div class="d">
                    <div class="e">
                        <div class="f"></div>
                        <div class="g"></div>
                        <div class="t t1"></div>
                        <div class="t t2"></div>
                        <div class="t t3"></div>
                        <div class="t t4"></div>
                        <div class="t t5"></div>
                        <div class="t t6"></div>
                        <div class="t t7"></div>
                        <div class="p">
                            <div class="pw">
                                <div class="pi">
                                    <div class="pl"></div>
                                </div>
                                <div class="pi">
                                    <div class="pr"></div>
                                </div>
                            </div>
                        </div>
                    </div>
```

```
                                        </div>
                                    </div>
                                </div>
                            </div>
                        </div>
                    </div>

        <div class="ys" style="width:50%">
            <div class="a">
                <div class="b">
                    <div class="c">
                        <div class="d">
                            <div class="e">
                                <div class="f"></div>
                                <div class="g"></div>
                                <div class="t t1"></div>
                                <div class="t t2"></div>
                                <div class="t t3"></div>
                                <div class="t t4"></div>
                                <div class="t t5"></div>
                                <div class="t t6"></div>
                                <div class="t t7"></div>
                                <div class="p">
                                    <div class="pw">
                                        <div class="pi">
                                            <div class="pl"></div>
                                        </div>
                                        <div class="pi">
                                            <div class="pr"></div>
                                        </div>
                                    </div>
                                </div>
                            </div>
                        </div>
                    </div>
                </div>
            </div>
        </div>
```

CSS

```css
/* borders and background */
.ys .a {padding:1.5%;
    -moz-border-radius:100% 100% 0 0 / 166% 166% 0 0;
    -webkit-border-top-left-radius:1000em;
    -webkit-border-top-right-radius:1000em;
    border-radius:100% 100% 0 0 / 166% 166% 0 0;
    background: #b0b4b7;
    background: -moz-linear-gradient(left, #b0b4b7 8%, #3f3f40 54%);
    background: -webkit-gradient(linear, left top, right top, color-stop(8%,#b0b4b7),
     color-stop(54%,#3f3f40));
    background: -webkit-linear-gradient(left, #b0b4b7 8%,#3f3f40 54%);
    background: -o-linear-gradient(left, #b0b4b7 8%,#3f3f40 54%);
    background: -ms-linear-gradient(left, #b0b4b7 8%,#3f3f40 54%);
    filter: progid:DXImageTransform.Microsoft.gradient(startColorstr='#b0b4b7',
```

```
        endColorstr='#3f3f40',GradientType=1);
    background: linear-gradient(left, #b0b4b7 8%,#3f3f40 54%);
}


.ys .b {padding:5% 5% 0 5%;
    -moz-border-radius:100% 100% 0 0 / 166% 166% 0 0;
    -webkit-border-top-left-radius:1000em;
    -webkit-border-top-right-radius:1000em;
    border-radius:100% 100% 0 0 / 166% 166% 0 0;
    background: #dadadc;
    background: -moz-linear-gradient(left, #dadadc 8%, #3a3a3c 54%);
    background: -webkit-gradient(linear, left top, right top, color-stop(8%,#dadadc),
     color-stop(54%,#3a3a3c));
    background: -webkit-linear-gradient(left, #dadadc 8%,#3a3a3c 54%);
    background: -o-linear-gradient(left, #dadadc 8%,#3a3a3c 54%);
    background: -ms-linear-gradient(left, #dadadc 8%,#3a3a3c 54%);
    filter: progid:DXImageTransform.Microsoft.gradient( startColorstr='#dadadc',
     endColorstr='#3a3a3c',GradientType=1 );
    background: linear-gradient(left, #dadadc 8%,#3a3a3c 54%);
}


.ys .c {padding:2.5% 2.5% 0 2.5%;
    -moz-border-radius:100% 100% 0 0 / 166% 166% 0 0;
    -webkit-border-top-left-radius:1000em;
    -webkit-border-top-right-radius:1000em;
    border-radius:100% 100% 0 0 / 166% 166% 0 0;
    background: #e1e4e5;
    background: -moz-linear-gradient(left, #e1e4e5 8%, #010204 54%);
    background: -webkit-gradient(linear, left top, right top, color-stop(8%,#e1e4e5),
     color-stop(54%,#010204));
    background: -webkit-linear-gradient(left, #e1e4e5 8%,#010204 54%);
    background: -o-linear-gradient(left, #e1e4e5 8%,#010204 54%);
    background: -ms-linear-gradient(left, #e1e4e5 8%,#010204 54%);
    filter: progid:DXImageTransform.Microsoft.gradient( startColorstr='#e1e4e5',
     endColorstr='#010204',GradientType=1 );
    background: linear-gradient(left, #e1e4e5 8%,#010204 54%);
}


.ys .d {padding:2%; background-color:#0c1c48;
    -moz-border-radius:100% 100% 0 0 / 166% 166% 0 0;
    -webkit-border-top-left-radius:1000em;
    -webkit-border-top-right-radius:1000em;
    border-radius:100% 100% 0 0 / 166% 166% 0 0;
}


.ys .e {padding:58% 5% 0 5%; position:relative; overflow:hidden;
    -moz-border-radius:100% 100% 0 0 / 166% 166% 0 0;
    -webkit-border-top-left-radius:1000em;
    -webkit-border-top-right-radius:1000em;
    border-radius:100% 100% 0 0 / 166% 166% 0 0;
    background: #394d97;
    background: -moz-linear-gradient(left, #394d97 8%, #282963 54%);
    background: -webkit-gradient(linear, left top, right top, color-stop(8%,#394d97),
     color-stop(54%,#282963));
    background: -webkit-linear-gradient(left, #394d97 8%,#282963 54%);
```

```
    background: -o-linear-gradient(left, #394d97 8%,#282963 54%);
    background: -ms-linear-gradient(left, #394d97 8%,#282963 54%);
    filter: progid:DXImageTransform.Microsoft.gradient( startColorstr='#394d97',
     endColorstr='#282963',GradientType=1 );
    background: linear-gradient(left, #394d97 8%,#282963 54%);
}

/* glare */
.ys .f {padding:50% 56%; position:absolute; top:11%; left:0;
    -moz-border-radius:166% 133% 0 0 / 166% 139% 0 0;
    -webkit-border-top-left-radius:166em 166em;
    -webkit-border-top-right-radius:133em 139em;
    border-radius:166% 133% 0 0 / 166% 139% 0 0;
    background: #2c3e90;
    background: -moz-linear-gradient(left, #2c3e90 8%, #120744 54%);
    background: -webkit-gradient(linear, left top, right top, color-stop(8%,#2c3e90),
     color-stop(54%,#120744));
    background: -webkit-linear-gradient(left, #2c3e90 8%,#120744 54%);
    background: -o-linear-gradient(left, #2c3e90 8%,#120744 54%);
    background: -ms-linear-gradient(left, #2c3e90 8%,#120744 54%);
    filter: progid:DXImageTransform.Microsoft.gradient( startColorstr='#2c3e90',
     endColorstr='#120744',GradientType=1 );
    background: linear-gradient(left, #2c3e90 8%,#120744 54%);
}

/* base */
.ys .g {padding:50% 74%; position:absolute; bottom:-135%; left:-16%;
    -moz-border-radius:100%;
    -webkit-border-radius:1000em;
    border-radius:100%;
    background: #99c1e2;
    background: -moz-linear-gradient(top, #99c1e2 1%, #7aaed9 3%, #2f6bb0 12%);
    background: -webkit-gradient(linear, left top, left bottom, color-stop(1%,#99c1e2),
     color-stop(3%,#7aaed9), color-stop(12%,#2f6bb0));
    background: -webkit-linear-gradient(top, #99c1e2 1%,#7aaed9 3%,#2f6bb0 12%);
    background: -o-linear-gradient(top, #99c1e2 1%,#7aaed9 3%,#2f6bb0 12%);
    background: -ms-linear-gradient(top, #99c1e2 1%,#7aaed9 3%,#2f6bb0 12%);
    filter: progid:DXImageTransform.Microsoft.gradient( startColorstr='#99c1e2',
     endColorstr='#2f6bb0',GradientType=0 );
    background: linear-gradient(top, #99c1e2 1%,#7aaed9 3%,#2f6bb0 12%);
}

/* ticks */
.ys .t {width:14%; height:6%; background-color:#e7e8e9; position:absolute;
    -moz-border-radius:30% / 100%;
    -webkit-border-radius:1000em;
    border-radius:30% / 100%;
}
.ys .t1 {left:7%; bottom:18%;}
.ys .t2 {left:11%; bottom:47%;
    -webkit-transform:rotate(30deg);
    -moz-transform:rotate(30deg);
    -o-transform:rotate(30deg);
    -ms-transform:rotate(30deg);
    transform:rotate(30deg);
```

```
}
.ys .t3 {left:24%; bottom:70%;
    -webkit-transform:rotate(60deg);
    -moz-transform:rotate(60deg);
    -o-transform:rotate(60deg);
    -ms-transform:rotate(60deg);
    transform:rotate(60deg);
}
.ys .t4 {left:44%; top:16%;
    -webkit-transform:rotate(90deg);
    -moz-transform:rotate(90deg);
    -o-transform:rotate(90deg);
    -ms-transform:rotate(90deg);
    transform:rotate(90deg);
}
.ys .t5 {right:24%; bottom:70%;
    -webkit-transform:rotate(-60deg);
    -moz-transform:rotate(-60deg);
    -o-transform:rotate(-60deg);
    -ms-transform:rotate(-60deg);
    transform:rotate(-60deg);
}
.ys .t6 {right:11%; bottom:47%;
    -webkit-transform:rotate(-30deg);
    -moz-transform:rotate(-30deg);
    -o-transform:rotate(-30deg);
    -ms-transform:rotate(-30deg);
    transform:rotate(-30deg);
}
.ys .t7 {right:7%; bottom:18%;}

/* pointer by @thierrykoblentz */
.ys .p {padding-bottom:52%; width:11%; position:absolute; left:50%; bottom:20%;
 margin-left:-5%;
    -webkit-transform:rotate(20deg);
    -moz-transform:rotate(20deg);
    -o-transform:rotate(20deg);
    -ms-transform:rotate(20deg);
    transform:rotate(20deg);
    -webkit-transform-origin:bottom;
    -webkit-transition:all 200ms cubic-bezier(0.200, 0.000, 1.000, 0.360);
}
.ys:hover .p {
    -webkit-transform:rotate(90deg);
    -moz-transform:rotate(90deg);
    -o-transform:rotate(90deg);
    -ms-transform:rotate(90deg);
    transform:rotate(90deg);
}
.ys .pw {position:absolute; top:0; right:0; bottom:0; left:0;}
.ys .pw > :first-child {border-right:1px solid transparent; margin-right:-2px;}
.ys .p::after {content:""; position:absolute; width:97%; padding-bottom:92%; top:88%;
 z-index:1;
    -moz-border-radius:100%;
    -webkit-border-radius:1000em;
```

```
      border-radius:100%;
      background: #ef4d58;
      background: -moz-linear-gradient(left, #ef4d58 10%, #ce1f2b 20%);
      background: -webkit-gradient(linear, left top, right top, color-stop(10%,#ef4d58),
       color-stop(20%,#ce1f2b));
      background: -webkit-linear-gradient(left, #ef4d58 10%,#ce1f2b 20%);
      background: -o-linear-gradient(left, #ef4d58 10%,#ce1f2b 20%);
      background: -ms-linear-gradient(left, #ef4d58 10%,#ce1f2b 20%);
      filter: progid:DXImageTransform.Microsoft.gradient(startColorstr='#ef4d58',
       endColorstr='#ce1f2b',GradientType=1);
      background: linear-gradient(left, #ef4d58 10%,#ce1f2b 20%);
}
.ys .pi {width:50%; height:100%; overflow:hidden; position:relative; float:left;}
.ys .pl, .ys .pr {position:absolute; width:200%; height:120%; left:50%;
      -webkit-transform:rotate(10deg);
      -moz-transform:rotate(10deg);
      -o-transform:rotate(10deg);
      -ms-transform:rotate(10deg);
      transform:rotate(10deg);
      background: #ef4d58;
      background: -moz-linear-gradient(left, #ef4d58 10%, #ce1f2b 20%);
      background: -webkit-gradient(linear, left top, right top, color-stop(10%,#ef4d58),
       color-stop(20%,#ce1f2b));
      background: -webkit-linear-gradient(left, #ef4d58 10%,#ce1f2b 20%);
      background: -o-linear-gradient(left, #ef4d58 10%,#ce1f2b 20%);
      background: -ms-linear-gradient(left, #ef4d58 10%,#ce1f2b 20%);
      filter: progid:DXImageTransform.Microsoft.gradient( startColorstr='#ef4d58',
       endColorstr='#ce1f2b',GradientType=1 );
      background: linear-gradient(left, #ef4d58 10%,#ce1f2b 20%);
}
.ys .pr {right:50%; left:auto;
      -webkit-transform:rotate(-10deg);
      -moz-transform:rotate(-10deg);
      -o-transform:rotate(-10deg);
      -ms-transform:rotate(-10deg);
      transform:rotate(-10deg);
}
```

CHAPTER 12

Useless Downloads of Background Images in Android

Éric Daspet

Let's begin with a quick reminder. In CSS, the "C" stands for "cascading." You may specify many conflicting rules for an element property: only one will be applied, based on different weights and priorities.

```
p { background-image: url(red.png) }
p { background-image: url(green.png) }
p.intro { background-image: url(yellow.png) }
```

With the previous code and a `<p class=intro>`, your paragraph should be displayed with a yellow background. Browsers are smart. If you don't have any other `<p>` tag, they will only download the yellow image and even if you do, the red image will never be downloaded.

The Android Problem

Well... that's how it *should* work. WebKit had an old bug fixed in late 2010 (*https://bugs.webkit.org/show_bug.cgi?id=24223*) that made it download all three images. In a complex website, this could be a major performance glitch.

Why am I digging up an old bug? Chrome, Safari, and other webkit-based browsers are probably up-to-date by now, but our problem still lives in the mobile world: Android. Almost every default browser shipped in Android 2.x device is still affected by this performance issue.

The mobile world is highly fragmented and updates are not regularly scheduled. Looking at Android smartphones, the majority of devices is still running under Android 2.2 or Android 2.3. Some devices, like the Nexus S, will probably be updated to Android 4.0 in the first quarter of 2012. However, sadly, most of them won't. You will still find Android 2.2 and 2.3 devices for years. For example, here in France, the Samsung Galaxy

S was a true success but it will be running Android 2.3, and will still be used for at least one year, maybe two.

If you target a mobile audience, you now know one of your performance enemies. If you don't... well, it seems that you have bigger problems to deal with.

And the Lack of Solution

You probably expect a happy ending to this note with a solution, or at least some workaround. You are right to expect this, but I won't be able to help.

As far as I know, there is no workaround, so here are two guidelines:

- Add background images in your CSS only to #id selectors.
- Avoid using multiple selectors with background images that may target the same element (which means style sheet without cascade).

I know, these guidelines are impossible to follow without exceptions. The purpose here is not to remove all useless downloads, but to reduce them with a "best effort" rule, in order to help your user experience. At the very least, try to avoid using the cascade for large background images that span the entire web page.

 To comment on this chapter, please visit *http://calendar.perfplanet.com/ 2011/useless-downloads-of-background-images-in-android/*. Originally published on Dec 12, 2011.

CHAPTER 13

Timing the Web

Alois Reitbauer

Analyzing the loading behavior of web pages by using browser plug-ins like YSlow, SpeedTracer or dynaTrace Ajax Edition has become really easy. As soon as we leave the browser, the story however is a different one. Getting detailed data from real users is much harder and only possible to a certain level of granularity. The usual approach is to use synthetic monitoring and execute tests from a variety of points of presence as close to end users as possible. If you measure from many locations and cover most of your transactions, this comes pretty close to the users' perceived performance. In case you are interested in more details on the pros and cons of using synthetic monitoring, recommend this blog post (*http://blog.dynatrace.com/2011/10/06/is-synthetic-monitor ing-really-going-to-die/*).

The best way however to understand the performance from a user's perspective is to measure in the actual browser. While this sounds very simple, it turns out to rather be a challenge. Creating a waterfall chart like the one on Figure 13-1 by just using information available in the browser simply is impossible.

Although there are free libraries like Boomerang (*https://github.com/yahoo/boomer ang*) and commercial products that can provide some of this information, it tends to be pretty tough. Actually of the first question that comes up is one of the hardest to answer: How long does it take to load a page. Let's be more precise here. How long does it take from the time a user initiates the loading of a page by clicking a link or typing a URL until the page is fully loaded. This—with some inaccuracies—is still doable for subsequent pages however impossible for start pages. What however is already possible is today using a small portion of JavaScript as shown in Example 13-1, which will calculate the time from the beginning of the page until it is loaded. While this provides a hint on loading times, we do not see DNS lookups, the establishment of connection or redirects. So these values might or might not reflect the load time perceived by the user.

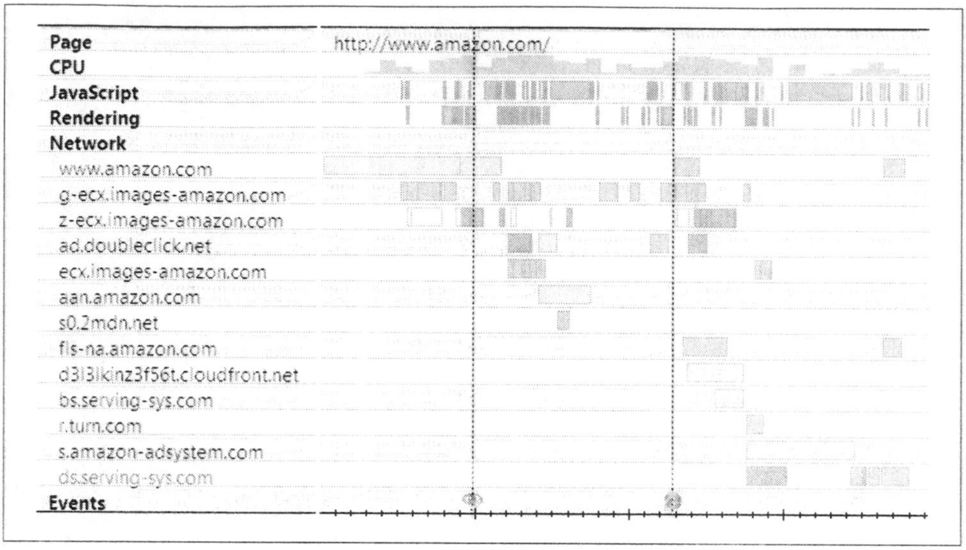

Figure 13-1. Waterfall chart showing client activity in the browser

Example 13-1. Simple script for measuring page load time

```
<html>
  <head>
  <script>
    var start = new Date().getTime();
    function onLoad() {
       var now = new Date().getTime();
       var latency = now - start;
       alert("page loading time: " + latency);
    }
  </script>
  </head>
  <body onload="onLoad()">
  ...
```

If we now go even further and also want to time resources on the page like images, CSS, or JavaScript files, it gets even harder. We could use a code snippet like the one in Example 13-2 to get resource timings. The impact on the page load time as well as the effort for coding this behavior is significant.

Example 13-2. Simple approach to time resources with significant impact on load behaviour

```
...
<script>
  downloadStart("myimg");
</script>
<img src="./myimg.jpg" onload="downloadEnd('myimg')" />
...
```

So it is really hard to get performance information from an end user perspective. However, browsers have all this information. Wouldn't it be the most natural thing for a browser to do to expose it so that it can be easily accessed by JavaScript. This is what the W3C Web Performance Working Group (*http://www.w3.org/2010/webperf/*) is working on. The group is working on a set of standards which enable developers to get access to this data. Using the short piece of JavaScript in Example 13-3 we can easily find out how long it took to load a page.

Example 13-3. Using Navigation Timing to measure page load time

```
<html>
<head>
<script>
function onLoad() {
  var now = new Date().getTime();
  var page_load_time = now - performance.timing.navigationStart;
  alert("User-perceived page loading time: " + page_load_time);
}

</script>
</head>
<body onload="onLoad()">
...
```

We can get even more details on the loading of a page to understand how long each "phase" of the page-loading process took. As shown on Figure 13-2, we can find out how long it took to resolve the host name, establish a connection, send the request, and wait for the response or how long it took to execute onLoad handlers.

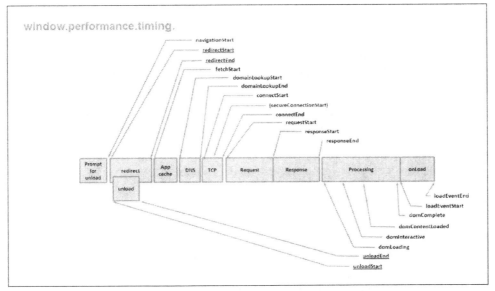

Figure 13-2. Detailed timings provided by Navigation Timing

Figure 13-3. Using Navigation Timing in desktop and mobile browsers

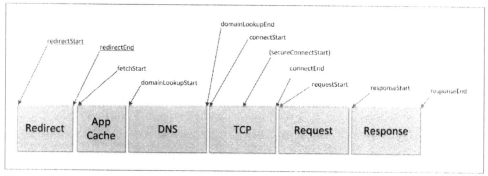

Figure 13-4. Timings provided by resource timings

This functionality, called Navigation Timing (*http://w3c-test.org/webperf/specs/Naviga tionTiming/*), is already implemented in latest browser versions. On mobile, IE9 on Windows Mango already exposes this information as well (Figure 13-3).

Although this is a great step forward, we still lack a significant amount of details about page loading behavior. Most importantly, we miss details about downloaded resources. Everything that happens between the start of the response and the onLoad event stays a black box.

Therefore the Resource Timing (*http://w3c-test.org/webperf/specs/ResourceTiming/*) specification defines an interface to access detailed networking information about resources. Just as with the initial page, we get the same granularity of information as for the main document (Figure 13-4).

Unfortunately this spec is not yet implemented in current browsers but hopefully will be available with future browser versions by mid next year. I think this is true at least for all the browsers that already implement Navigation Timing.

So this gives us great insight into the networking behavior of the application; what we still miss however is the ability to time custom events on a page. Let's look at a simple example. Assume we want to measure when certain content is visible on the page. This is where the User Timing specification (*http://w3c-test.org/webperf/specs/ResourceTiming/*) comes into play. User Timing allows us to measure discrete points in time, like how long it took from navigation start to the displaying of certain content on a page. The snippet in Example 13-4 shows how this code might look like.

Example 13-4. Measuring a custom point in page load using User Timing

```
var perf = window.performance;
perf.measure("customLoad");
var customLoadTime = perf.getMeasures("customLoad")[0];
```

So putting all this together, we have a good way to time all major events that happen on a page. Because using all these different APIs might end up being a bit confusing, there will also be a common interface to access all this data. That's what the Performance Timeline (*http://w3c-test.org/webperf/specs/UserTiming/*) is about. The timeline provides a unified interface to access all performance-related information.

Conclusion

While they are not fully implemented yet, the new W3C specifications for timing web pages provide an easy way to access performance information right in the user's browsers. In future browser versions we will be able to drop a lot of the magic code used today to get end user timing information.

A question that however stays unanswered is how this data is sent back to the server. Currently there are two possible approaches. We can use beacons (HTTP GET request that piggyback the monitoring data) or XHRs. Both approaches work acceptably well in most cases; there are some issues with sending data in the onBeforeUnload event. So if we put everything together and add server-side infrastructure this is the data we can collect about our end users.

As a final sneak peek, I can show you what level of granularity we will get using modern technology. The information on Figure 13-5 is collected by our own monitoring using a kind of "backport" of Navigation and Resource Timing into existing browsers.

If you want to try it the new APIs today, just follow this link (*http://blog.dynatrace.com/samples/bookmark.html*) and check how long it took to load this page. You can use this simple bookmarklet to get timing information for any page you are interested in.

 To comment on this chapter, please visit *http://calendar.perfplanet.com/2011/timing-the-web/*. Originally published on Dec 13, 2011.

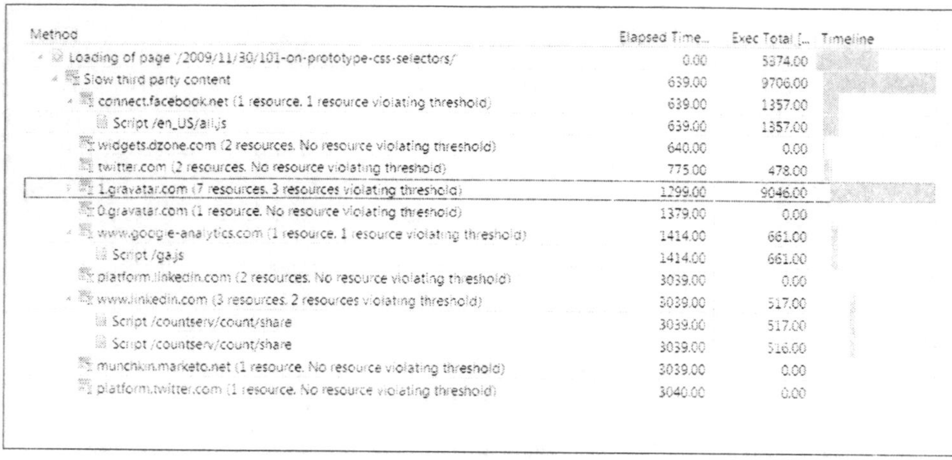

Method	Elapsed Time...	Exec Total [...	Timeline
◢ ▣ Loading of page '/2009/11/30/101-on-prototype-css-selectors/'	0.00	5374.00	
◢ ▤ Slow third party content	639.00	9706.00	
◢ ▤ connect.facebook.net (1 resource. 1 resource violating threshold)	639.00	1357.00	
▤ Script /en_US/all.js	639.00	1357.00	
▤ widgets.dzone.com (2 resources. No resource violating threshold)	640.00	0.00	
▤ twitter.com (2 resources. No resource violating threshold)	775.00	478.00	
▤ 1.gravatar.com (7 resources. 3 resources violating threshold)	1299.00	9046.00	
▤ 0.gravatar.com (1 resource. No resource violating threshold)	1379.00	0.00	
◢ ▤ www.google-analytics.com (1 resource. 1 resource violating threshold)	1414.00	661.00	
▤ Script /ga.js	1414.00	661.00	
▤ platform.linkedin.com (2 resources. No resource violating threshold)	3039.00	0.00	
◢ ▤ www.linkedin.com (3 resources. 2 resources violating threshold)	3039.00	517.00	
▤ Script /countserv/count/share	3039.00	517.00	
▤ Script /countserv/count/share	3039.00	516.00	
▤ munchkin.marketo.net (1 resource. No resource violating threshold)	3039.00	0.00	
▤ platform.twitter.com (1 resource. No resource violating threshold)	3040.00	0.00	

Figure 13-5. End-user-based performance data for a blog page showing slow third parties

CHAPTER 14

I See HTTP

Stoyan Stefanov

Ladies and gentlemen, boys and girls. Say hello to `icy`.

icy

It's an iOS app that lets you debug HTTP. It's like HTTPWatch (*http://httpwatch .com/*) or WebPagetest (*http://webpagetest.org/*), but for mobile. Like blaze.io's mobit-est (*http://www.blaze.io/mobile/*), but in your pocket, it works with 3G, Edge (as these can have different characteristics and carrier optimizations than WiFi), and also lets you inspect pages behind login.

Some details

- It's a `UIWebView` that loads the page you want and provides a `NSURLCache` class, which logs whatever the iOS networking layer throws at it.
- It's on github (*https://github.com/stoyan/icy*). Note that this is my very first attempt at iOS and Obj-C so the code quality is probably atrocious. License is public do-main, because I don't really understand the others.
- The name is `icy`, because it's iOS and *it's the law* that app names be prefixed with an "i". Also (to my Eastern European ear at least), "icy" sounds like "I see" (spelled "ic" in chats) and is the beginning of (said with spookiest of voices) "I see... HTTPeee."

Walkthrough

A journey of a thousands miles begins with a single tap. As you can see in Fig-ure 14-1, the icon is the default/missing icon. (Who cares about icons?) If you focus

Figure 14-1. App icon

hard enough you may convince yourself that the white icon actually makes sense, it's like snow, or, there you have it, ice.

What we have then (Figure 14-2) is a **UIWebView** waiting to load a page and an address bar. Right there you already see the first problem with the app—**UIWebView** is not really iOS Safari. It may act differently and even have a different JavaScript engine. But it's as close as we can get.

Tapping, typing, tapping, typing... (See Figure 14-3.)

Oh look, a page is loaded! Now let's remove the veil and peek to see what's underneath all that fanciness (Figure 14-4).

Figure 14-2. The "browser"

Ha! Requests! (See Figure 14-5.)

As you can see, I stole the JS/CSS/HTML icons from the webkit project. And if a page component looks like an image (has `Content-Type: image/*`), you see a little thumbnail.

You see the number of requests that this page made.

Also each request line is a link to more details (Figure 14-6).

The details are split into "Meta," "Request headers," and "Response Headers." *Meta* contains general information such as URL and duration.

Figure 14-3. Navigating to a page

"But is the duration accurate?" you may ask as a critical reader and a performance geek. To the best of my knowledge it's pretty accurate.

Figure 14-7 shows request headers, as we know and love them.

If the text is cut off, you can tap again and get the full text of the header value (Figure 14-8).

After request/response headers, what we have is a preview of what the component looks like. If it's an image, you get a little thumbnail that you can click to get a bigger image (Figure 14-9, Figure 14-10).

Figure 14-4. Page loaded, waiting to be inspected

If the component is text, you get the first few characters and then tap for the real deal. (Figure 14-11, Figure 14-12)

And that's all there is for now.

Todos

There are a few immediate todos (for which I'd gladly take any help) and some more general ideas for going forward.

Figure 14-5. List of page components

First of all, is the NSURLCache (*http://developer.apple.com/library/mac/#documentation/ Cocoa/Reference/Foundation/Classes/NSURLCache_Class/Reference/Reference.html*) the best/only way to inspect the network? At first I was a little disappointed that the iOS SDK doesn't provide APIs to inspect the traffic. But then I saw what Patrick Meenan needs to do to make WebPagetest happen (*http://calendar.perfplanet.com/2011/webpa getest-internals/*), so I guess a little hacking and method swizzling (*http://www.cocoadev .com/index.pl?MethodSwizzling*) might be appropriate. Which might lower the chances of the app ever hitting the app store.

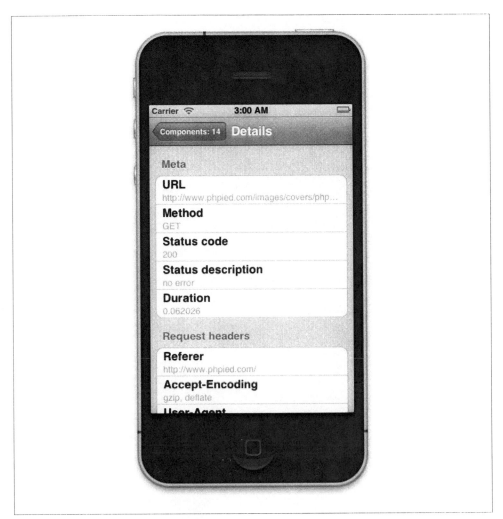

Figure 14-6. Component details view

Anyway, `NSURLCache` is a way to implement your own caching in your native/hybrid app. Which in and of itself is a nice optimization to know about when building iOS apps. You create a class extending `NSURLCache` and announce it:

```
[NSURLCachesetSharedURLCache:mycache];
```

And then every time the web view is about to make a request, it will ask your class "hey, got that google.com/logo.png thing?" And also every time a component is downloaded, it will be passed to your class so you can store it.

And this is how the `icy` app was built, only instead of storing and returning files, I just log anything that comes my way.

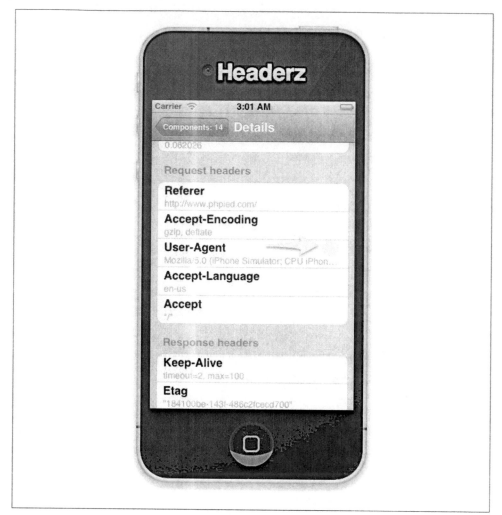

Figure 14-7. Request headers

And this "anything that comes my way" is where incompleteness of introspection comes in. Sometimes the networking layer doesn't call my method to say that a new response has arrived. Responses that are thought of as uncacheable may never reach my `NSURLCache` child. In these cases, you see in the app that I got the request, but no response for it to match. In the example in Figure 14-13 it's the PHP for Facebook's Like button. The white icon means I didn't get a `Content-Type` response header to inspect.

That's why I thought a refetch might be a good idea for inspecting URLs that we didn't get a response for. We can make a separate deliberate request and get the response, we

Figure 14-8. Full text of a header

don't rely on the `NSURLCache` and `UIWebView`. That's the idea and it's a todo currently (Figure 14-14).

The other thing is clearing the log (Figure 14-15). That's easy, but clearing the cache didn't prove to be so easy. I swear I did it at some point and it was working (I had to destroy the UIWebView to make it work), but then I changed something else and it stopped working. The change I suspect is when I deleted the *.xib/.nib* file I originally had for the UIWebView.

Figure 14-9. Component preview (images)

The Road Ahead

The road ahead is around HAR.

As you can see we can look at requests/responses, but it would be nice also to have things like a yslow score, page speed score, potential wins of minification, etc.—a bunch of tools. My idea is to separate the tools of performance intelligence from the mechanics of collecting the raw data. And the glue is HAR.

We have the online HAR viewer (*http://www.softwareishard.com/har/viewer/*) so no need to build waterfall diagrams, just pass it a HAR file.

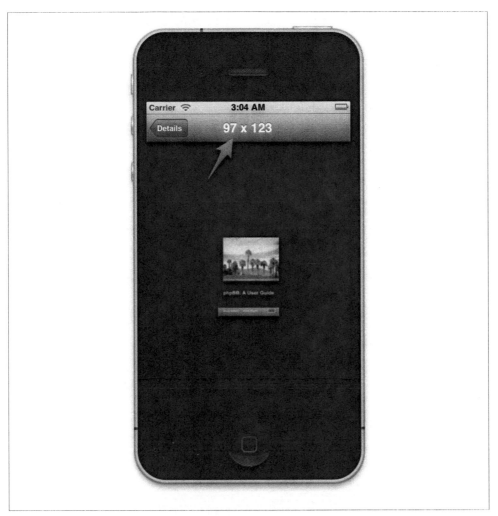

Figure 14-10. Component full view (images)

We now have a YSlow command line, which will be a question of time to get a Web UI going. It should accept a HAR and run all the YSlow intelligence on it. Same for PageSpeed. I shouldn't have to integrate all tools in `icy` but rather have `icy` open Safari, point to a URL of a tool, and pass it a HAR. Needless to say tool URLs should be configurable so you can run your own, even in-house, tools.

What `icy` can help address is the visibility into the `UIWebView`. Just getting the best data possible, creating a HAR and passing it on. This is what I call the mechanics of gathering the raw data, the "it is what it is" data. As opposed to the intelligence of tools like YSlow that can answer the question: "I have this page here, so what next?"

Figure 14-11. Component preview (text components, e.g. CSS, JS)

And I'm hoping we, the web performance community, will have these little lightweight "agents" on every possible device that makes network requests, so we can gather the raw HTTP data and pass it to the good old tools for their opinions. We also need to know what possible optimizations carriers do. So...

All I Want for Christmas...

...is more tools. We can only improve what we know about. Therefore visibility into what's going on is critical.

Figure 14-12. Component full view (text components)

This little `icy` app is just an example, sort of saying to manufacturers, phone builders, browser vendors—here's what we want, now gimme!

To comment on this chapter, please visit *http://calendar.perfplanet.com/ 2011/i-see-http/*. Originally published on Dec 14, 2011.

Figure 14-13. Missing response information

Figure 14-14. Refetch

Figure 14-15. Clearing log and browser cache

CHAPTER 15

Using Intelligent Caching to Avoid the Bot Performance Tax

Matthew Prince

In 2004, Lee Holloway (*https://twitter.com/icqheretic*) and I started Project Honey Pot (*http://www.projecthoneypot.org/*). The site, which tracks online fraud and abuse, primarily consists of web pages that report the reputation of IP addresses. While we had limited resources and tried to get the most of them, I just checked Google which lists more than 31 million pages in its index that make up the www.projecthoneypot.org (*http://www.projecthoneypot.org/*) site.

Project Honey Pot's pages are relatively simple and asset-light, but like many sites today they include significant dynamic content that is regularly updated at unpredictable intervals. To deliver near realtime updates, the pages need to be database driven.

To maximize performance of the site, from the beginning we used a number of different caching layers to store the most frequently accessed pages. Lee, whose background is high-performance database design, studied reports from services like Google Analytics to understand how visitors moved through the site and built caching to keep regularly accessed pages from needing to hit the database.

We thought we were pretty smart but, in spite of following the best practices of web application performance design, with alarming frequency the site would grind to a halt. The culprit turned out to be something unexpected and hidden from the view of many people optimizing web performance: automated bots.

The average website sees more than 20% of its requests coming from some sort of automated bot. These bots include the usual suspects like search engine crawlers, but also include malicious bots scanning for vulnerabilities or harvesting data. We've been tracking this data at CloudFlare across hundreds of thousands of sites on our network and have found that on average, approximately 15% of web total requests originate a web threat of one form or another (*http://blog.cloudflare.com/do-hackers-take-the-holi days-off*), with swings up and down depending on the day (Figure 15-1)

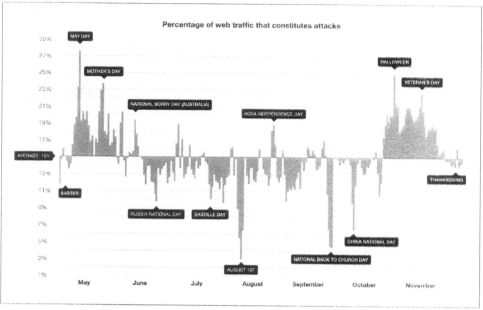

Figure 15-1. Attack of the holidays

In Project Honey Pot's case, the traffic from these bots had a significant performance impact. Because they did not follow the typical human visitation pattern, they were often triggering pages that weren't hot in our cache. Moreover, since the bots typically didn't fire Javascript beacons like those used in systems like Google Analytics, their traffic and its impact weren't immediately obvious.

To solve the problem, we implemented two different systems to deal with two different types of bots. Because we had great data on web threats, we were able to leverage that to restrict known malicious crawlers from requesting dynamic pages on the site. Just taking off the threat traffic had an immediate impact and freed up database resources for legitimate visitors.

The same approach didn't make sense for the other type of automated bots: search engine crawlers. We wanted Project Honey Pot's pages to be found through online searches, so we didn't want to block search engine crawlers entirely. However, in spite of removing the threat traffic, Google, Yahoo, and Microsoft's crawlers all accessing the site at the same time would sometimes cause the web server and database to slow to a crawl.

The solution was a modification of our caching strategy. While we wanted to deliver the latest results to human visitors, we began serving search crawlers from a cache with a longer time to live (TTL). We experimented with the right TTLs for pages, but eventually settled on 1 day as being optimal for the Project Honey Pot site. If a page is crawled by Google today and then Baidu requests the same page less in the next 24 hours, we return the cached version without regenerating the page from the database.

Search engines, by their nature, see a snapshot of the Internet. While it is important to not serve deceptively different content to their crawlers, modifying your caching strategy to minimize their performance impact on your web application is well within the bounds of good web practices.

Since starting CloudFlare (*https://www.cloudflare.com/*), we've taken the caching strategy we developed at Project Honey Pot and made it more intelligent and dynamic to optimize performance. We automatically tune the search crawler TTL to the characteristics of the site, and are very good at keeping malicious crawlers from ever hitting your web application. On average, we're able to offload 70% of the requests from a web application — which is stunning given the entire CloudFlare configuration process takes about 5 minutes. While some of this performance benefit comes from traditional CDN-like caching, some of the biggest cache wins actually come from handling bots' deep page views that aren't alleviated by traditional caching strategies.

The results can be dramatic. For example, SXSW's website employs extensive traditional web application and database caching systems but was able to reduce the load on their web servers and database machines by more than 50% (*http://blog.cloudflare.com/cloudflare-powers-the-sxsw-panel-picker*) in large part because of CloudFlare's bot-aware caching (Figure 15-2).

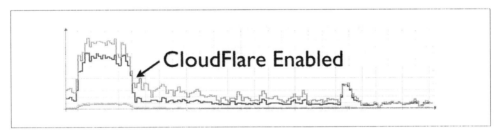

Figure 15-2. Bot-aware caching results

When you're tuning your web application for maximum performance, if you're only looking at a beacon-based analytics tool like Google Analytics you may be missing one of the biggest sources of web application load. This is why CloudFlare's analytics reports the visits from all visitors to your site. Even without CloudFlare, digging through your raw server logs, being bot-aware, and building caching strategies that differentiate between the behaviors of different classes of visitors can be an important aspect of any site's web performance strategy.

 To comment on this chapter, please visit *http://calendar.perfplanet.com/2011/using-intelligent-caching-to-avoid-the-bot-performance-tax/*. Originally published on Dec 15, 2011.

CHAPTER 16

A Practical Guide to the Navigation Timing API

Buddy Brewer

Navigation Timing (*http://dvcs.w3.org/hg/webperf/raw-file/tip/specs/NavigationTim ing/Overview.html*) is an API from the W3C's Web Performance Working Group (*http: //www.w3.org/2010/webperf/*) that exposes data about the performance of your web pages. Navigation Timing is a major new development because it enables you to collect fine-grained performance metrics from real users, including events that happen before Javascript-based trackers have a chance to load. This gives us the ability to directly measure things like DNS resolution, connection latency, and time to first byte *from inside the browsers of real users.*

Why You Should Care

I spent the first eight years of my career building synthetic monitoring products but I now believe real user monitoring should be your preferred source of "The Truth" when it comes to understanding the performance of your site. That doesn't mean you should throw away your synthetic monitoring, but today I view it as a useful complement to real user monitoring rather than a complete performance solution in itself.

Real user monitoring is critical because it provides the most accurate portrayal of the true experience across the browsers, locations, and networks your users are on. It is the only way to realistically measure how your caching decisions impact the user experience. Measuring real people (with real personalities and real credit cards) also gives you an opportunity to collect performance and business metrics in the same context, so you can see what impact load times are having on key business metrics like conversion and bounce rates.

The biggest problem we face with Navigation Timing is that there isn't a good system for collecting and analyzing the raw data. In this chapter, I'll describe a solution to this problem that can be quickly deployed using free tools.

Collecting Navigation Timing Timestamps and Turning Them into Useful Measurements

The `window.performance.timing` object gives all of its metrics in the form of timestamps relative to the epoch. In order to turn these into useful measurements, we need to settle on a common vocabulary and do some arithmetic. I suggest starting with the following:

```
function getPerfStats() {
  var timing = window.performance.timing;
  return {
    dns: timing.domainLookupEnd - timing.domainLookupStart,
    connect: timing.connectEnd - timing.connectStart,
    ttfb: timing.responseStart - timing.connectEnd,
    basePage: timing.responseEnd - timing.responseStart,
    frontEnd: timing.loadEventStart - timing.responseEnd
  };
}
```

This gives you a starting point that is similar to the waterfall components you commonly see in synthetic monitoring tools. It would be interesting to collect this data for a while and compare it to your synthetic data to see how close they are.

Using Google Analytics as a Performance Data Warehouse

Next we need a place to store the data we're collecting. You could write your own beacon service or simply encode the values on a query string, log them in your web server's access logs, and write a program to parse and analyze the results. However these are time-consuming approaches. We're looking for something we can get up and running quickly and at minimal cost. Enter Google Analytics (*http://www.google.com/analytics/*).

Google Analytics is the most popular free web site analytics system on the Internet. While GA automatically provides basic performance metrics in its Site Speed Analytics Report (*http://analytics.blogspot.com/2011/05/measure-page-load-time-with-site-speed .html*), it is based on a sample of data and only reports on the total page load time. We can improve this by using GA's event tracking capability to store and analyze our fine-grained Navigation Timing metrics:

```
window.onload = function() {
  if (window.performance && window.performance.timing) {
    var ntStats = getPerfStats();
    _gaq.push(["_trackEvent", "Navigation Timing", "DNS", undefined, ntStats.dns, true]);
    _gaq.push(["_trackEvent", "Navigation Timing", "Connect", undefined, ntStats.connect, true]);
    _gaq.push(["_trackEvent", "Navigation Timing", "TTFB", undefined, ntStats.ttfb, true]);
    _gaq.push(["_trackEvent", "Navigation Timing", "BasePage", undefined, ntStats.basePage, true]);
    _gaq.push(["_trackEvent", "Navigation Timing", "FrontEnd", undefined, ntStats.frontEnd, true]);
  }
};
```

The preceding code fires five events to transmit our five performance measurements. We are waiting until the load event to ensure we get a valid measurement of the front end time. If we weren't concerned with front end performance, we could fire the events at any point during page load. The final **true** parameter in each call is important to ensure that the events don't get misinterpreted by Google Analytics as user interactions, which would skew bounce rate calculations.

For more information see the Google Analytics Event Tracking Guide (*http://code.goo gle.com/apis/analytics/docs/tracking/eventTrackerGuide.html*).

Reporting on Performance in Google Analytics

Now that we've collected our Navigation Timing data in Google Analytics, it's time to run some reports. Log into Google Analytics and click *Content→Events→Top Events*. Click on *Navigation Timing* under the Event Category list and GA displays a table showing the number of measurements and average value for each of our five performance dimensions. This view also lets you plot the average value of any of the five dimensions over time (Figure 16-1).

Event Action		Total Events	↓	Unique Events	Event Value	Avg. Value
1.	BasePage	6		3	4	0.67
2.	Connect	6		3	150	25.00
3.	DNS	6		3	47	7.83
4.	FrontEnd	6		3	2,857	476.17
5.	TTFB	6		3	188	31.33

Figure 16-1. Example Google Analytics Report

Limitations

This approach has the advantage of being quick to set up using freely available tools and techniques. But as with most things that are fast and cheap, it has a few shortcomings:

Lack of browser coverage

Navigation Timing isn't yet available in Safari (desktop or mobile) and obviously won't be available in legacy versions of browsers that will be around for some time to come. Testing with a subset of browsers is probably fine for measuring conditions before the page starts getting parsed, but when you begin looking at frontend performance the lack of data from certain browsers has a bigger impact.

No object level data

Synthetic monitoring still rules the roost here. The W3C Resource Timing (*http://dvcs.w3.org/hg/webperf/raw-file/tip/specs/ResourceTiming/Overview.html*) specification promises to provide object level data from real users in the future, but as of this writing it isn't available in any popular browsers.

Limited to the capabilities of the Google Analytics reporting system

With Google Analytics, you have to take what you're given. You can generate and plot averages of measurements, but you won't get percentiles, degradation alerts, or many other features you are accustomed to seeing from performance monitoring tools.

Final Thoughts

Now that Navigation Timing is available in the top three browsers, everyone should have some form of real user monitoring in their performance toolbox. The approach outlined above isn't perfect but it gives you a basic level of coverage at no cost and minimal effort.

My company, Log Normal (*http://www.lognormal.com/*), is building a premium real user monitoring solution that aims to give you the best possible insight into real user performance. If you're interested in learning more, head over to our website, and request a beta invitation (*http://www.lognormal.com/*).

 To comment on this chapter, please visit *http://calendar.perfplanet.com/2011/a-practical-guide-to-the-navigation-timing-api/*. Originally published on Dec 16, 2011.

CHAPTER 17

How Response Times Impact Business

Alexander Podelko

It looks like there is great interest to quantifying performance impact on business, linking response time to income and customer satisfaction. A lot of information was published, for example, the Aberdeen Group report, "Customers Are Won or Lost in One Second (*http://dev.gomez.com/wp-content/downloads/Aberdeen_WebApps.pdf*)", or the Gomez whitepaper "Why Web Performance Matters: Is Your Site Driving Customers Away? (*http://www.gomez.com/pdfs/wp_why_web_performance_matters.pdf*)" There is no doubt that there is a strong correlation between response times and business metrics and it is very good to have such documents to justify performance engineering efforts —and some simplification may be good from the practical point of view—but we should keep in mind that the relationship is not so simple and linear and there may be cases when it would matter.

Response times may be considered as usability requirements and are based on the basic principles of human-computer interaction. As long ago as 1968, Robert Miller's paper "Response Time in Man-Computer Conversational Transactions" described three threshold levels of human attention. Jakob Nielsen believes that Miller's guidelines are fundamental for human-computer interaction (*http://www.useit.com/papers/response time.html*), so they are still valid and not likely to change with whatever technology comes next. These three thresholds are:

- Users view response time as instantaneous (0.1-0.2 second)
- Users feel they are interacting freely with the information (1-5 seconds)
- Users are focused on the dialog box (5-10 seconds)

Users view response time as instantaneous (0.1-0.2 seconds): Users feel that they directly manipulate objects in the user interface. For example, the time from the moment the user selects a column in a table until that column highlights or the time between typing a symbol and its appearance on the screen. Robert Miller reported that threshold as 0.1 seconds. According to Peter Bickford 0.2 seconds forms the mental boundary between events that seem to happen together and those that appear as echoes of each other (*http://web.archive.org/web/20040913083444/http://developer.netscape.com/viewsource/bickford_wait.htm*).

Although it is a quite important threshold, it is often beyond the reach of application developers. That kind of interaction is provided by operating system, browser, or interface libraries, and usually happens on the client side, without interaction with servers (except for dumb terminals, that is rather an exception for business systems today). However new rich web interfaces may make this threshold important for consideration. For example, if there is logic processing user input so screen navigation or symbol typing becomes slow, it may cause user frustration even with relatively small response times.

Users feel they are interacting freely with the information (1-5 seconds): They notice the delay, but feel that the computer is "working" on the command. The user's flow of thought stays uninterrupted. Robert Miller reported this threshold as one-two seconds.

Peter Sevcik identified two key factors impacting this threshold (*http://www.netforecast.com/Articles/BCR%20C26%20How%20Fast%20is%20Fast%20Enough.pdf*): the number of elements viewed and the repetitiveness of the task. The number of elements viewed is, for example, the number of items, fields, or paragraphs the user looks at. The amount of time the user is willing to wait appears to be a function of the perceived complexity of the request.

Back in 1960s through 1980s, the terminal interface was rather simple and a typical task was data entry, often one element at a time. So earlier researchers reported that one to two seconds was the threshold to keep maximal productivity. Modern complex user interfaces with many elements may have higher response times without adversely impacting user productivity. Users also interact with applications at a certain pace depending on how repetitive each task is. Some are highly repetitive; others require the user to think and make choices before proceeding to the next screen. The more repetitive the task is the better the response time should be.

That is the threshold that gives us response time usability goals for most user-interactive applications. Response times above this threshold degrade productivity. Exact numbers depend on many difficult-to-formalize factors, such as the number and types of elements viewed or repetitiveness of the task, but a goal of two to five seconds is reasonable for most typical business applications.

There are researchers who suggest that response time expectations increase with time. Forrester research of 2009 (*http://www.akamai.com/html/about/press/releases/2009/press_091409.html*) suggests two second response time; in 2006 similar research suggested four seconds (both research efforts were sponsored by Akamai, a provider of web accelerating solutions). While the trend probably exists (at least for the Internet and mobile applications, where expectations changed a lot recently), the approach of this research was often questioned because they just asked users. It is known that user perception of time may be misleading. Also, as mentioned earlier, response time expectations depends on the number of elements viewed, the repetitiveness of the task, user assumptions of what the system is doing, and interface interactions with the user. Stating a standard without specification of what page we are talking about may be overgeneralization.

Users are focused on the dialog box (5-10 seconds): They keep their attention on the task. Robert Miller reported threshold as 10 seconds. Users will probably need to reorient themselves when they return to the task after a delay above this threshold, so productivity suffers. Or, if we are talking about Web sites, it is the threshold when users start abandoning the site.

Peter Bickford investigated user reactions when, after 27 almost instantaneous responses, there was a 2 minute wait loop for the 28th time for the same operation (*http://web .archive.org/web/20040913083444/http://developer.netscape.com/viewsource/bickford _wait.htm*). It took only 8.5 seconds for half the subjects to either walk out or hit the reboot. Switching to a watch cursor during the wait delayed the subject's departure for about 20 seconds. An animated watch cursor was good for more than a minute, and a progress bar kept users waiting until the end. Bickford's results were widely used for setting response times requirements for web applications.

That is the threshold that gives us response time usability requirements for most user-interactive applications. Response times above this threshold cause users to lose focus and lead to frustration. Exact numbers vary significantly depending on the interface used, but it looks like response times should not be more than 8 to 10 seconds in most cases. Still, the threshold shouldn't be applied blindly; in many cases, significantly higher response times may be acceptable when appropriate user interface is implemented to alleviate the problem.

So while there is a strong correlation between response times and business metrics, it is definitely not a linear function. We are touching on the psychology of human-computer interaction and it is definitely not a single-dimension issue. It is very context-specific and published data should be used carefully with understanding what really stands behind them. The main practical conclusion is that you may have a point when further performance improvement won't make much sense: you have increasing costs of performance improvement with diminishing business value. Although it looks like most existing systems haven't reached this point yet.

 To comment on this chapter, please visit *http://calendar.perfplanet.com/ 2011/how-response-times-impact-business/*. Originally published on Dec 17, 2011.

CHAPTER 18

Mobile UI Performance Considerations

Estelle Weyl

The mobile segment is the fastest growing segment of Internet users. If your site is accessible via the mobile browser, you'll notice that your mobile OS stats has been increasing rapidly. Developing with mobile in mind will improve user experience on all devices, not just phones. Whether or not you design for mobile first (*http://www.lukew.com/ff/entry.asp?933*), you definitely need to consider mobile performance when developing web applications.

Mobile devices may have browsers that are similar to, or even more featured, than the browsers on personal computers. Even with more advanced browsers, the devices themselves may have similar memory and bandwidth constraints to the Pentium III you were using back in 1999. While your users may be using similar applications to access your sites, the devices themselves create various constraints that you need to consider during development.

When it comes to mobile, you need to take battery life, latency, memory, and UI responsiveness into consideration throughout the development process.

Battery Life

Mobile users are just that: mobile. Unlike desktop computers which are tethered to the wall at all times, and even laptop computers which are generally used by stationary users, mobile users do not recharge their devices throughout the day. Mobile users expect their devices to last at least 24 hours between recharging.

While most users realize that calls and GPS usage consume battery power, they don't realize that different websites will drain their battery faster than other sites. You may have noticed that CPU usage drains the battery on your laptop when unplugged. CPU usage drains the battery on your mobile device just as effectively! Manage CPU usage. Avoid repaints. Minimize both size and activity of your JavaScript. Always use CSS, rather than JavaScript for animations. And, even when supported, never serve WebGL to a mobile device.

Anything that makes your laptop churn, warm up, or turn your computer's fan on also drains the battery if you're not plugged in. Remember, your mobile device users are not plugged in!

Latency

Download and upload speeds are NOT equal to the bandwidth marketed by ISPs. The quoted MBps is actually the *fastest* connection one could possibly ever hope to get. The speed by which a website, including the markup, stylesheets, media, application scripts, and third-party scripts, makes it onto our devices impacted almost as much by latency as by the bandwidth of the marketing terms of Edge or 3G.

We won't dive into latency here. If you want a better understanding of latency and bandwidth in general, check out *An Engineer's Guide to Bandwidth* (*http://developer .yahoo.com/blogs/ydn/posts/2009/10/a_engineers_gui/*) by Tom Hughes-Croucher (*http://twitter.com/sh1mmer*). (It also describes some tips on reducing packets.)

"Mobile users have terrible latency, so a site optimized for mobile should really reduce the number of HTTP requests it makes. Note that mobile users that surf the Web over WiFi experience far lower latency." — Phillip Tellis (*http://www.yuiblog.com/blog/ 2010/04/08/analyzing-bandwidth-and-latency/*)

What is important to know is that latency has a much larger impact on download speeds on mobile devices than on tethered devices or devices accessing the Internet via WiFi. Actual speeds have more to do with packet loss and latency. Air—the stuff packets go thru to get from a mobile device to a cell tower—is the main cause of latency. In other words, your mobile users using 3/4G already have low bandwidth. Latency makes their web surfing experience that much more painful.

Because of latency issues, reducing DNS lookups and HTTP requests is vital in the mobile space. This leads us to the first web performance optimization anti-pattern: embedding stylesheets and scripts.

Embedding CSS and JS: A Best Practice?

Best practices for speeding up your website (*http://developer.yahoo.com/performance/ rules.html*) recommend making your JavaScript and CSS files external and using a content delivery network, or CDN. However, external files mean more http requests, and using CDNs for static content adds both more DNS look ups and more http requests. While embedding CSS and JS in your HTML goes against all best practices I've ever espoused, if done correctly, embedding your scripts on first load can help improve performance. Bing's mobile website is a perfect example (Figure 18-1, Figure 18-2).

As pointed by Nicholas Zakas (*http://www.slideshare.net/nzakas/mobile-web-speed -bumps*), when you access m.bing.com (*http://m.bing.com/*) for the first time from your mobile device, the entire site loads as a single file. The CSS and JS are embedded. Images

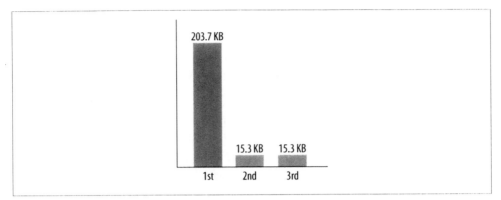

Figure 18-1. First download is 203.7 KB, following download is 15.3

Figure 18-2. Screenshot of bing's mobile website

are included at data URIs. Bing for mobile put all their assets into a single file necessitating only a single http request. However, that single file is 200KB. That is huge. However, only the first visit to Bing returns such a large file. By taking advantage of localStorage and cookies, every subsequent request to m.bing.com returns a single file of manageable size. While the first request returns a huge file, every subsequent request produces a response of about 15KB.

Bing embeds all the files needed into the single HTML file. Using client-side JavaScript, Bing extracts the CSS, JS, and images from the original download, and saves the CSS, JS, and image data URIs in local storage. Bing saves the names of the stored files in a cookie. With every subsequent page request, the cookie informs the server which files are already saved locally, allowing the server to determine which assets, if any, need to be included in the response. In this way, subsequent responses only include scripts, styles, and images not saved in local storage, if any, along with the HTML.

The steps to reducing the negative effects of latency in a mobile site download by making a web app with a single HTTP request for all HTML, CSS, JS, and images include the following steps:

- Embedding CSS & JS for first page load
- Extract and put the above embedded files in LocalStorage
- Set cookies with the names of the extracted embedded files
- On subsequent requests, check the cookies server side
- Only embed new and missing scripts based on cookie values
- Load files from localStorage resources on load

Note: If you're wondering why this method may be more efficient than simply downloading and caching files: not only does this method improve performance by avoiding the latency of multiple DNS lookups and HTTP requests, but mobile devices have more limited cache, with iOS having no persistent memory.

Pulling data out of localStorage is a performance hit (*http://calendar.perfplanet.com/ 2011/localstorage-read-performance/*). When it comes to mobile, however, it is less of a hit than latency, especially latency with limited bandwidth.

Memory

Most performance recommendation focus on improving I/O speeds. It is not sufficient to only focus on how long it takes for responses to complete in the mobile space. When it comes to mobile and the limited memory on most mobile devices, we have to also manage what happens *on* the device. As developers, we generally develop on our personal computers where memory is virtually unlimited. Mobile users, however, are running our sites on devices with very limited memory.

Memory on personal computers has increased almost exponentially over the past 2 decades. 256MB may have been more than enough to run all software on a Pentium II in 1997. In 2011, however, base model (i.e., "slow") computers come with at least 2GB of RAM. An iPhone 3G has 128MB of memory. The original iPad has 256MB. The faster HTC Inspire has 768MB. The norm for new, high-end smart phones is around 512MB of RAM with 1GHz processors. Mobile devices have software written in 2011, but run on devices that have the memory of a 1997 desktop.

While 512MB may seem large enough to run any web application, in managing memory it is important to remember that the browser (and web application) is not the only process consuming the limited RAM. The operating system, background processes, and other open applications (operating system and user initiated) are all sharing the memory. Mobile devices are generally running many native applications as well as user installed apps, with or without the users knowledge. Running applications are many, including user initiated apps like Twitter, GPS, Facebook, apps that came with the device but may be running unbeknownst to the user, like Calendar and Media, and applications downloaded by the user, like Angry Birds. Native OS applications and all apps with user notifications turned on continue to run in the background. A device with 512MB of RAM likely has less than 200MB of available memory. In managing memory, remember that your web application's most active users are likely also the ones using other mobile applications. When testing, test with real world devices. Run apps like Twitter, Facebook, and Mail with notifications on all your testing devices.

The greater the number of applications running on a device, the less memory available for your web application. And, even if none of those applications are memory hogs, the sheer number of apps running in the background creates high memory usage conditions. High memory usage causes a slow UI, and when the browser is out of memory, it is out of memory. The mobile browser will generally close or crash to free up memory. You need to manage the memory requirements of your web applications to ensure they don't slow or crash the mobile browser.

Optimize Images

Other than avoiding CSS expressions (YSlow) and Optimize images (PageSpeed), the performance optimization guidelines have to do with I/O and not what happens once the site is on the device. While gzipping files helps improve download speed it does not help with memory management. Once the asset is on the device, it is no longer compressed. Images use up memory. Images over 1024px cause greater memory issues. Reduce your image file sizes by serving up the image with the dimensions at which it will be displayed, and by compressing the image at that size. There are a few tools at your disposal. ImageAlpha (*http://pngmini.com/*) can help convert your transparent pngs into 8-bit pngs with full transparency. The Sencha.io (*http://www.sencha.com/ learn/how-to-use-src-sencha-io/*) proxy determines what size image the user's device requires and will shrink (not grow) images before sending them to the client.

While reducing image file size has always been important for web performance, when it comes to mobile, we can't focus only on the I/O file size. You have to consider how large the image file is uncompressed as memory is limited. All images use up memory. Composited images use GPU memory instead of CPU memory. So, while that may be a neat trick to free up some memory, composited images use up four times the memory of their non-composited counterparts, so use this trick sparingly.

I recommend keeping your web application files at use at any one time (JS, CSS, HTML, and images currently displayed) to under 80MB.

Weigh the Benefits of CSS

CSS can help reduce the number of HTTP requests and reduce the size of the requests that are made. With gradients, border-radius, box and text shadow, and border images, you can greatly reduce the number of HTTP requests. The benefits of CSS is that effects are:

- Requiring fewer HTTP requests
- Updatable
- Scalable
- Transitionable
- Animatable

However, painting these effects to the screen has associated costs. Sometimes pngs, gifs, and jpegs render faster and use less memory than CSS effects. Any CSS features that is transformable is generally evaluated at each reflow and repaint, using up memory. PNG, JPEG, and GIF images, unlike CSS-generated images, are rendered and transitioned as bitmaps, often using less memory (but more HTTP requests). For example, shadows, especially inset shadows, are kept in memory and are repainted even if obfuscated by another element with a higher z-index. And, while a radial gradient may take 140 characters of CSS, the browser will paint and keep in memory the entire gradient, not just the section of gradient that is displayed in the viewport. I recommend using linear gradients and native rounded corners over images, but weigh the performance of radial gradients and inset shadows against the cost of downloading image.

Weigh the benefits of CSS. While CSS images are generally the preferred solution over using PhotoShop and uploading exported pictures, some CSS features have hidden costs due to memory usage and rendering slowness.

GPU Benefits and Pitfalls

On some devices, by transitioning or transforming an element into a 3D space, the element is hardware accelerated (*http://www.html5rocks.com/en/tutorials/speed/html5/#toc-hardware-accell*). By transferring the rendering of the element from the CPU to the GPU, you can greatly improve performance, especially when animating. However, translate3D is not a panacea! Hardware-accelerated elements are composited. Composited elements take up four times the amount of memory. Using GPU instead of CPU will improve performance up to a point. While hardware-accelerated elements use up less RAM, they do use up video memory, so use the `div { transform: transla teZ(0); }` trick sparingly.

Viewport: Out of Sight Does Not Mean Out of Mind

The mobile phone viewport is the viewable screen area. Unlike your desktop browser where you scroll content, on mobile devices unless the viewport height and width are set, and scaling is disabled, the viewport is fixed and the user moves the content underneath. The viewport is a "port" through which your users view your content. Why is this a performance issue? Most don't realize that the content that is drawn to the page, even if it is not visible in the current viewport, is still in memory.

Minimize the DOM

Every time there is a reflow, every DOM node is measured. The CPU on your desktop can handle a virtually endless number of nodes (it will eventually crash). The memory on mobile devices is limited and garbage collection differs so is not fully reliable. To improve performance, minimize the number of nodes. Instead of allocating DOM nodes and destroying them (or forgetting to destroy them), pool and reuse your nodes. For example, if you're creating a card game, create no more than 52 nodes, reusing pooled nodes instead of creating a new node every time a card is added back into the game.

As you know from JavaScript best practices, touching the DOM with a read or write is expensive. Cache DOM lookups and store them in variables.

Also, batch DOM queries and DOM manipulations separately, minimizing DOM manipulations by updating content fully outside of the DOM before updating the DOM.

When it comes to managing memory, image optimization, CSS rendering, and DOM node count are not the only points of concern. These are just points that are not necessarily considered in the desktop space when focusing on performance.

UI Responsiveness

Mobile browsers are single threaded (*http://www.nczonline.net/blog/2010/08/10/what-is-a-non-blocking-script/*). In that respect, mobile browsers are similar to desktop browsers. Mobile devices are different though because of the limitations of the device. It is always important to manage your JavaScript. Bloated and inefficient JavaScript is even more problematic on mobile devices because of battery usage and memory.

There is more to UI responsiveness on mobile than just single-threaded-ness. Because of latency, the browser may appear to hang after selecting an action because it can take a while for the round trip. It is important to provide user feedback within 200ms after an action is taken. If you are showing or hiding an element, there's no need to provide feedback, since the app will be responsive. However, provide feedback to indicate that your site is responding if your user has to wait for a round trip for a UI update.

In addition, because the mobile device is a touch device, and "double tap" is a potential user action, mobile devices actually waits for potential double taps before responding to user action. On iOS devices there is a default 300ms wait after the touchend event before any action is taken. Because of this, you may want to co-opt default events like the tap with by adding an event listener to the touchend event to make your application more responsive.

Summary

The preceding is not an exhaustive list of topics to consider in ensuring good mobile UI performance, but should be a good start. Remember that mobile is the fastest increasing segment of our users. Don't ignore them.

As developers, we've tested our websites to make sure we've followed the points and goals recommended by Yahoo's YSlow, and Google's PageSpeed. We've tested and tested... using our desktop browsers. We've assumed the web performance optimization guidelines improves web application performance for all browsers, whether our users are accessing the site on their laptop, iPad, Android phone, or even their Wii. And, to a great extent, it does. But remember that the well known and heeded optimization guidelines aren't our only concern when it comes to mobile.

Do continue testing your website, but make sure to test on mobile devices. Emulators are not simulators. The emulator does not simulate memory constraints and does not simulate the device with 100 apps open. Test on real devices in real scenarios (turn the WiFi and test with many, many unclosed apps hanging in the background).

 To comment on this chapter, please visit *http://calendar.perfplanet.com/ 2011/mobile-ui-performance-considerations/*. Originally published on Dec 18, 2011.

CHAPTER 19

Stop Wasting Your Time Using the Google Analytics Site Speed Report

Aaron Peters

Since May 2011 the Site Speed report in Google Analytics shows how fast your pages load for your real visitors. Google Analytics measures page load time by using the Navigation Timing API (*http://w3c-test.org/webperf/specs/NavigationTiming/*) in all browsers that support it (IE9+, Chrome, FF7+, Android4+ (*http://caniuse.com/#search=nav igation*)) and falls back to Google Toolbar data for older versions of IE and Firefox. Having page speed data in GA is great, because you can easily correlate it to bounce rate and conversion, resulting in great, actionable insight that down the road leads to a faster site, happier users, and more revenues. But if a significant percentage of your visitors use Firefox 7 or 8, you may very well be wasting a lot of time interpreting the Site Speed data and even more time taking the wrong actions.

Problem: A Bug in Firefox Implementation of the Navigation Timing API

Firefox implemented the Navigation Timing API in version 7, which was released on September 27, 2011. From that day in that browser, there has been a bug in the implementation of that API. You can read all about it in the bug ticket (*https://bugzilla .mozilla.org/show_bug.cgi?id=691547*) on Bugzilla. The problem is that the value for `window.performance.timing.navigationStart` can be too low, which means it is too far in the past. Google Analytics uses a simple formula to calculate page load time: `loadTime = window.performance.timing.loadEventStart - window.performance.timing.naviga tionStart`. If `navigationStart` is too low, the page load time will be too high.

I see this bug affecting page load times in GA Site Speed report a lot. On one of my client's site, 27% of visitors use Firefox 7 or 8 and 24% use Chrome 15 or 16. The Site Speed report shows that the average page load time for Firefox users is 7.23 seconds and for Chrome it is 3.12 seconds. When zooming in on individual pages and dates, I often see that all the big spikes (30, 50, or 100+ seconds load times) are coming from Firefox. Never Chrome, never IE, always Firefox.

At least one commercial web application performance monitoring service provider has taken action on this bug. New Relic confirmed to me that they don't use the Navigation Timing API in Firefox to calculate page load time because it is not accurate.

So, what can you do to not have this bug mess up your data in GA?

Solution: Filter Out the Firefox Timings in Google Analytics

In Google Analytics, create a Custom Report and filter out all data from Firefox visitors (Figure 19-1).

Good News: The Bug Was Fixed in Firefox 9

Mozilla fixed the bug in Firefox 9, which was released on December 20, 2011 (*https://wiki.mozilla.org/Releases#Firefox_9*). Now that most visitors have upgraded to Firefox 12, you can remove the filter(s) in Google Analytics.

Closing Remark

You may already have known about this issue. In the Google Analytics Online Help, on this page (*http://support.google.com/analytics/bin/answer.py?hl=en&answer=1205784*), there is a note almost at the bottom of the page mentioning the Firefox bug. Google implies here that the bug has been impacting load times in the Site Speed report since November 16. I have no idea why. As far as I know, the bug has been in FF 7 from day one (September 27) and exists in Firefox 8 as well. In my opinion, the Google Analytics team should have written a blog post about this, and not merely mentioned it in the Online Help, where many GA users probably never look.

 To comment on this chapter, please visit *http://calendar.perfplanet.com/2011/stop-waisting-your-time-using-the-google-analytics-site-speed-report/*. Originally published on Dec 19, 2011.

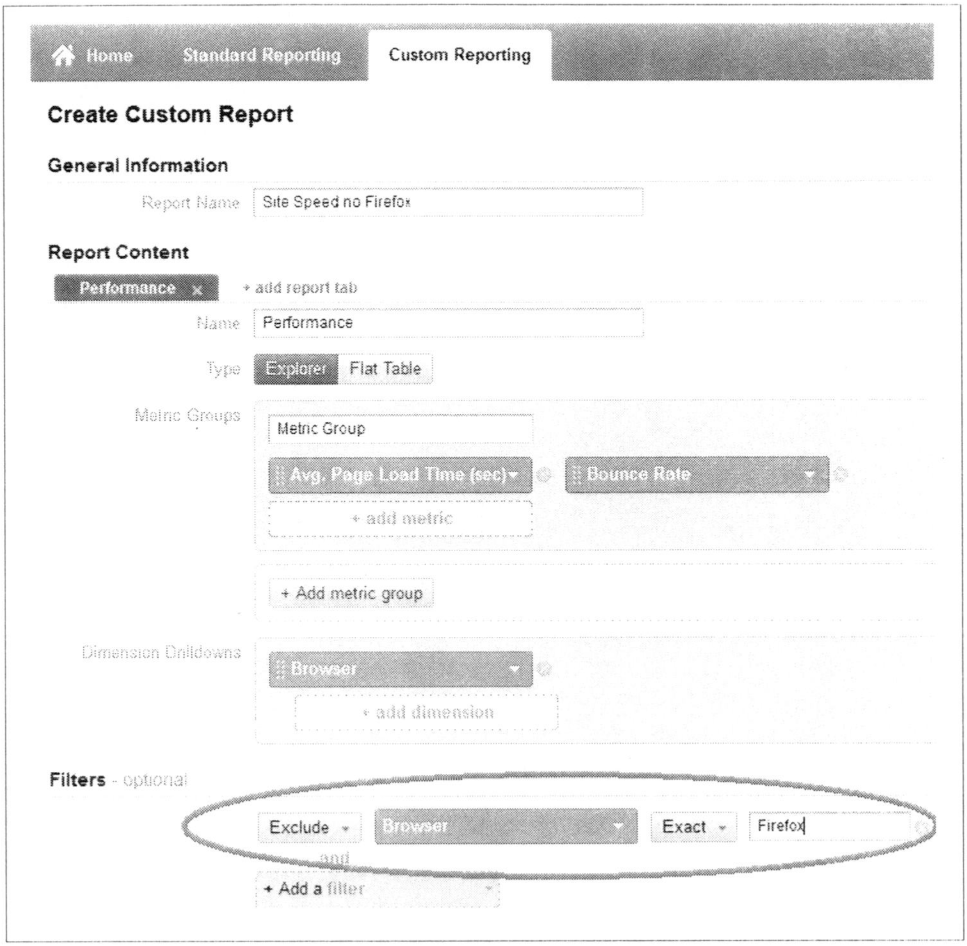

Figure 19-1. Custom Report in Google Analytics

CHAPTER 20

Beyond Web Developer Tools: Strace

Tony Gentilcore

Rich developer tools are available for all modern web browsers. They are typically easy to use and can provide all the information necessary to optimize web pages. It is rare to need to go beyond the unified networking/scripting/rendering view of the Web Inspector's Timeline panel (*http://www.webkit.org/blog/1091/more-web-inspector-up dates/#timeline_panel*).

But they aren't always perfect: a tool may be missing information, may disagree with another tool, or may just be incorrect. For instance, a recent bug (*https://bugs.webkit .org/show_bug.cgi?id=58354*) occasionally caused two Navigation Timing (*https://dvcs .w3.org/hg/webperf/raw-file/tip/specs/NavigationTiming/Overview.html*) metrics to be incorrect in Chrome (and the Inspector).

When these rare situations arise, great engineers are able to go beyond a browser's developer tools to find out exactly what the browser is telling the operating system to do. On Linux, this source of ultimate truth can be found using **strace**. This tool can trace each system call made by a browser. Since every network and file access entails a system call, and this is where browsers spend a lot of their time, it is perfect for debugging many types of browser performance issues.

What About Other Platforms?

In this post, I introduce strace because the syntax is clean and no setup is required. But most systems have an equivalent tool for tracing system calls. Mobile developers will be happy to hear that strace is fully supported by Android. OS X users will find **dtrace** offers more powerful functionality at the expense of less intuitive syntax (unfortunately not ported to iOS). Finally, *Event Tracing for Windows* (ETW), while harder to set up, supports a friendly GUI.

Getting Started

To use it: open a terminal and invoke `strace` at the command prompt. This invocation prints all system calls while starting Google Chrome to google.com:

```
$ strace -f -ttt -T google-chrome http://www.google.com/
```

I've added `-f` to follow `forks`, `-ttt` to print the timestamp of each call and `-T` to print the duration of each call.

Zeroing In

If you run the preceding command, you'll probably be overwhelmed by the amount of stuff going on in a modern web browser. To filter down to something interesting, try using the `-e` argument. For examining only file or network access, try `-e trace=file` or `-e trace=network`. The man page (*http://linux.die.net/man/1/strace*) has many more examples.

Example: Local Storage

As a concrete example, let's trace local storage performance in Chrome. First I opened a local storage quota test page (*http://arty.name/localstorage.html*). Then I retrieved the Chrome browser processes' ID from Chrome's task manager (Wrench > Tools > Task Manager) and attached strace to that process using the `-p` switch.

```
$ strace -f -T -p _<process id>_ -e trace=open,read,write
```

The output shows the timestamps, arguments and return value of every `open`, `read`, and `write` system call. The man page for each call explains the arguments and return values. The first call of interest to us is this `open`:

```
open("/home/tonyg/.config/google-chrome/Default/Local                Storage/
http_arty.name_0.localstorage-journal", O_RDWR|O_CREAT, 0640) = 114 <0.000391>
```

This shows us that Chrome has opened this file for reading and writing (and possibly created it). The name of the file is a big clue that this is where local storage is saved for arty's web page. The return value, `114`, is the file descriptor, which will identify it in later reads and writes. Now we can look for `read` and `write` calls which operate on fd 114, for example:

```
write(114,
"\0\0\00020\0001\0002\0003\0004\0005\0006\0007\0008\0009\0000\0001\0002\0003\0
"..., 1024 <unfinished ...> <... write resumed> ) = 1024 <0.425476>
```

These two lines show a 1,024 byte write of the data beginning with the string above to the local storage file (114). This write happened to take 425ms. Note that the call is split into two lines with possibly others in between because another thread preempted it. This is common for slower calls like this.

We've Only Scratched the Surface

There are options for dumping the full data read/written from the network or filesystem. Running with -c displays aggregate statistic about the time spent in the most common calls. I've also found that some practical python scripting can quickly parse these traces into a variety of useful formats.

This brief introduction hardly does this tool justice. I merely hope it provides the courage to explore deeper into the stack the next time you run into a tricky performance problem.

 To comment on this chapter, please visit *http://calendar.perfplanet.com/2011/beyond-web-developer-tools-strace/*. Originally published on Dec 20, 2011.

CHAPTER 21

Introducing mod_spdy: A SPDY Module for the Apache HTTP Server

Bryan McQuade and Matthew Steele

At Google, we strive to make the whole Web fast. Our work in this area includes Page Speed Online (*https://developers.google.com/pagespeed/*), mod_pagespeed (*http://code.google.com/p/modpagespeed/*), Page Speed Service (*http://code.google.com/speed/pss/*), Google Chrome (*https://www.google.com/chrome*), making TCP faster (*http://code.google.com/speed/articles/tcp_initcwnd_paper.pdf*), and the SPDY protocol (*http://dev.chromium.org/spdy/spdy-whitepaper*), among other efforts. The SPDY (pronounced "SPeeDY") protocol allows websites to be transmitted more efficiently to the web browser, resulting in page load time improvements (*http://blog.chromium.org/2009/11/2x-faster-web.html*) of as much as 55%. To make it easier for websites to realize the benefits of SPDY, we're releasing the source code for mod_spdy (*http://code.google.com/p/mod-spdy/*), an open-source module for the Apache HTTP server.

Getting Started with mod_spdy

mod_spdy is still in early beta, and is not yet recommended for deployment in production environments. If you'd like to test out mod_spdy and help us to make it better, please consult our Getting Started (*http://code.google.com/p/mod-spdy/wiki/GettingStarted*) guide. We hoped to make it production-ready sometime in early 2012. Stay tuned by subscribing to our discussion forum (*http://groups.google.com/group/mod-spdy-discuss*).

SPDY and Apache

mod_spdy is an Apache 2.2-compatible module that provides SPDY support for Apache HTTP servers. Multiplexing is an important performance feature of SPDY which allows for multiple requests in a single SPDY session to be processed concurrently, and their responses interleaved down the wire. However, due to the serialized nature of the HTTP/1.1 protocol, the Apache HTTP server provides a one-request-per-connection architecture. Apache's connection and request processing normally happens in a single thread, like shown on Figure 21-1.

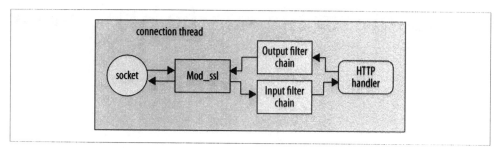

Figure 21-1. Apache's connection and request processing

This works well for HTTP, but it presents a problem for multiplexed protocols like SPDY because in this flow, each connection can only process one request at a time. Once Apache starts processing a request, control is transferred to the request handler and does not return to the connection handler until the request is complete.

To allow for SPDY multiplexing, mod_spdy separates connection processing and request processing into different threads. The connection thread is responsible for decoding SPDY frames and dispatching new SPDY requests to the mod_spdy request thread pool. Each request thread can process a different HTTP request concurrently. The diagram on Figure 21-2 shows the high-level architecture.

To learn more about how mod_spdy works within Apache, consult our wiki (*http://code.google.com/p/mod-spdy/wiki/HowItWorks*).

Help to Improve mod_spdy

You can help us to make mod_spdy better by doing compatibility and performance testing, by reviewing the code (*http://code.google.com/p/mod-spdy/source/browse/trunk/src#src%2Fmod_spdy%2Fcommon*) and sending us feedback on the mod_spdy discussion list (*https://groups.google.com/group/mod-spdy-discuss*). We look forward to your contributions and feedback!

   To comment on this chapter, please visit *http://calendar.perfplanet.com/2011/introducing-mod_spdy-a-spdy-module-for-the-apache-http-server/*. Originally published on Dec 21, 2011.

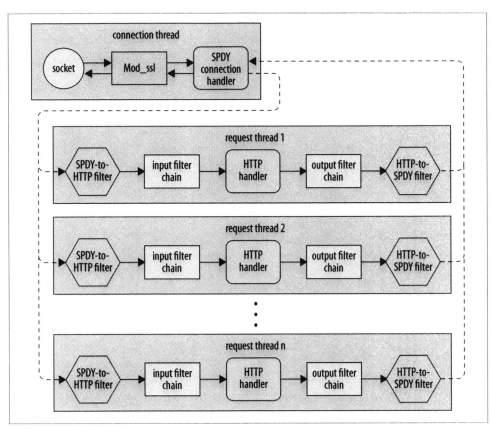

Figure 21-2. High-level architecture

CHAPTER 22

Lazy Evaluation of CommonJS Modules

Tobie Langel

About two years ago, the mobile Gmail team posted an article focused on reducing the startup latency (*http://googlecode.blogspot.com/2009/09/gmail-for-mobile-html5-series -reducing.html*) of their HTML5 application. It described a technique which enabled bypassing parsing and evaluation of JavaScript until it was needed by placing it inside comments. Charles Jolley (*http://www.okito.net/*) of SproutCore (*http://sproutcore .com/*) fame was quick to jump on the idea. He experimented with it (*http://blog.sprout core.com/faster-loading-through-eval/*) and found that similar performance gains could be achieved by putting the code inside of a string rather then commenting it. Then, despite promises (*http://www.okito.net/post/8409610016/on-sproutcore-2-0*) of building it into SproutCore, this technique pretty much fell into oblivion. That's a shame because it's an interesting alternative to lazy loading that suits CommonJS modules really well.

Close Encounters of the Text/JavaScript Type

To understand how this technique works, let's look at what happens when the browser's parser encounters a `script` element with a valid `src` attribute. First, a request is sent to the server. Hopefully the server responds and the browser proceeds to download (and cache) the requested file. Once these steps are completed, the file still needs to be parsed and evaluated (Figure 22-1).

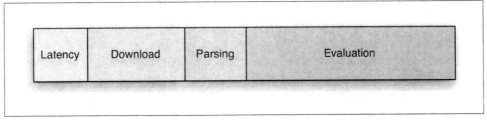

Figure 22-1. Uncached JavaScript resource fetching, parsing, and evaluation

For comparison, Figure 22-2 shows the same request hitting a warm HTTP cache.

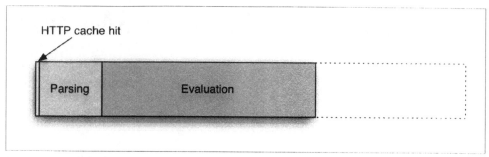

Figure 22-2. Cached JavaScript resource fetching, parsing, and evaluation

What's worth noticing here—other than the obvious benefits of caching—is that parsing and evaluation of the JavaScript file still happen on every page load, regardless of caching. While these steps are blazing fast on modern desktop computers, they aren't on mobile. Even on recent, high-end devices. Consider the graph in Figure 22-3, which compares the cost of parsing and evaluating jQuery on the iPhone 3, 4, 4S, iPad, iPad 2, a Nexus S, and a MacBook Pro. (Note that these results are indicative only. They were gathered using the test hosted at lazyeval.org (*http://lazyeval.org/*), which at this point is still very much alpha.)

Remember that these times come on top of whatever networking costs you're already facing. Furthermore, they'll be incurred on *every single page load*, regardless of whether or not the file was cached. Yes, you're reading this right. On an iPhone 4, parsing and evaluating jQuery takes over 0.3 seconds, *every single time the page is loaded*. Arguably, those results have substantially improved with more recent devices, but you can't count on your whole user base owning last generation smartphones, can you?

Lazy Loading

A commonly suggested solution to the problem of startup latency is to load scripts on demand (for example, following a user interaction). The main advantage of this technique is that it delays the cost of downloading, parsing, and evaluating until the script is needed. Note that in practice—and unless you can delay *all* your JavaScript files— you'll end up having to pay round trip costs twice (Figure 22-4).

There are a number of downsides to this approach, however. First of all, the code isn't guaranteed to be delivered: the network or the server can become unavailable in the meantime. Secondly, the speed at which the code is transferred is subject to the network's quality and can thus vary widely. Lastly, the code is delivered asynchronously. These downsides force the developer to build both defensively and with asynchronicity in mind, irremediably tying the implementation to it's delivery mechanism in the process. Unless the whole codebase is built on these premises—which is probably

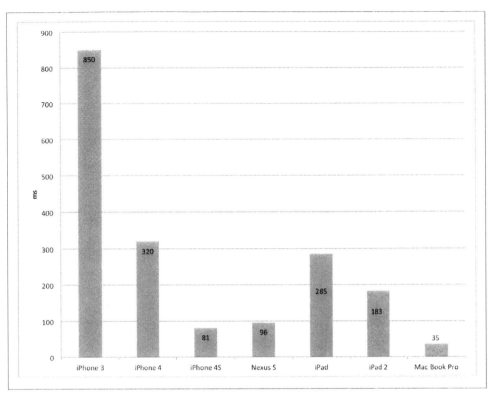

Figure 22-3. Parsing and evaluating jQuery

something you want to avoid—deferring the loading of a chunk of code becomes a non-trivial endeavor.

Lazy Evaluation to the Rescue

Lazy evaluation avoids these issues altogether by focusing on delaying the parsing and evaluation stages only. The script can be either bundled with the initial payload or inlined. It is prevented from being evaluated during initial page load by being either commented-out or escaped and turned into a string ("stringified"?). In both cases, the content is simply evaluated when required (Figure 22-5).

And again, for comparison, hitting a warm HTTP cache is shown on (Figure 22-6)

As the graph of an iPad 2 parsing and evaluating jQuery shows (Figure 22-7), both options consistently out-perform regular evaluation by at least a factor of ten. Similar tenfold performance improvements were observed on all tested devices.

Commented-out code has slightly better performance indices than "stringified" code does. It can however be quite complicated to extract when not inlined. It is also more brittle: some phone operators are known to strip out JavaScript comments

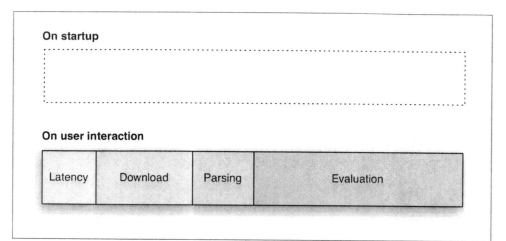

Figure 22-4. Lazy-loading JavaScript

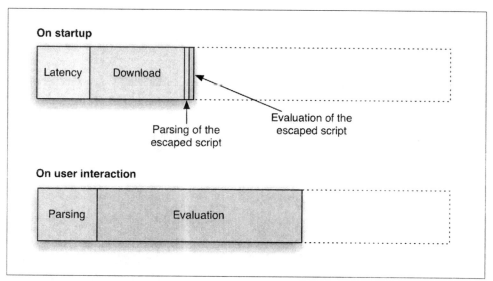

Figure 22-5. Lazy evaluation

(*http://www.mysociety.org/2011/08/11/mobile-operators-breaking-content/*). "Stringi-fied" code, on the other hand is both more robust and a lot easier to access, that's why its preferred.

Building Lazy Evaluation into CommonJS Modules

It turns out that the CommonJS module's (http://wiki.commonjs.org/wiki/Modules/ 1.1) extra level of indirection (the `require` call) makes it an ideal candidate for lazy

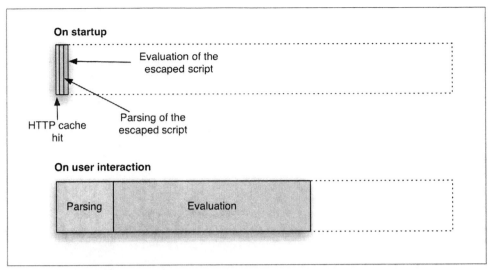

On startup

Evaluation of the
escaped script

HTTP cache
hit

Parsing of the
escaped script

On user interaction

Parsing

Evaluation

Figure 22-6. Lazy evaluation of a cached script

evaluation. Since lazy evaluation is synchronous, the whole process can be made completely transparent to the developer. Enabling lazy evaluation becomes a one-liner in a config file, not a large architectural change. Even better, the dependency graph built through static analysis can be leveraged to automatically lazy evaluate all the selected module's dependencies.

Implementation-wise, enabling lazy evaluation of CommonJS modules requires modifying the runtime so that it correctly evaluates and wraps modules which are transported in their "stringified" form. In modulr (*https://github.com/tobie/modulr-node/*), my CommonJS module dependencies resolver, this is done like so (*https://github.com/ tobie/modulr-node/blob/v0.6.1/assets/modulr.sync.js#L26-29*):

```
if (typeof fn === 'string') {
  fn = new Function('require', 'exports', 'module', fn);
}
```

This implies lazy evaluated modules be escaped (*https://github.com/tobie/modulr-node/ blob/v0.6.1/lib/collector.js#L56-61*) and surrounded by quotes (*https://github.com/to bie/modulr-node/blob/v0.6.1/lib/collector.js#L76*) at build time on the server-side, before transport.

The initial results are promising, but at this point, it is merely work in progress. Future plans for modulr include enabling full minification of it's output (just minifying the output won't do as it would miss modules transported as strings), instrumenting the runtime to be able to gather perf data and experimenting with a Souders-inspired per module localStorage cache (*http://www.stevesouders.com/blog/2011/09/26/app-cache -localstorage-survey/*). If there's interest, I'd also like to automate lazyeval.org (*http:// lazyeval.org/*) to allow it to measure performance gain of applying this technique onto

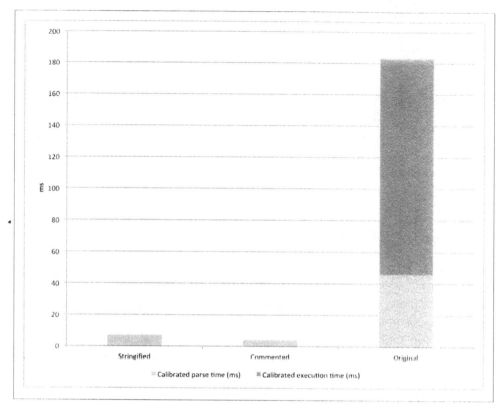

Figure 22-7. Parsing and evaluating jQuery in Pad 2

other JavaScript libraries and reporting those results to browserscope.org (*http://www .browserscope.org/*).

 To comment on this chapter, please visit *http://calendar.perfplanet.com/ 2011/lazy-evaluation-of-commonjs-modules/*. Originally published on Dec 22, 2011.

CHAPTER 23

Advice on Trusting Advice

Billy Hoffman

We all know that third-party content means you no longer control all the factors which affect page load time. A sleek, well-tuned, and optimized site can still deliver a poor user experience because of problems with third-party content. Steve Souders even used to publish a series of blog posts (*http://stevesouders.com/p3pc/*) where he analyzed and rated the performance of third-party content snippets (*http://www.stevesouders.com/ blog/2010/02/17/performance-of-3rd-party-content/*). (*Dear Steve, please bring this back, it was awesome*). Mathias Bynens took this one step further, showing how to additionally optimize Google's markup and JavaScript snippets (*http://mathiasbynens .be/notes/async-analytics-snippet*).

The surprising lesson to learn from Steve and Mathias is that if you want a fast site *and* third-party widgets, then you need to examine the third-party content for performance problems, *even when a snippet comes from a trusted authority on web performance*. So this post isn't really going to be about third-party content. It's going to be about trusting advice.

Last week a Zoompf customer, the online precious metal exchange GoldMoney (*http: //goldmoney.com/*), contacted Support about an issue our technology flagged on their site. We had detected an issue with Google's JavaScript library for their Google+ button. Zoompf WPO was suggesting the customer do something which was contradicting Google's advice. And that was enough to give GoldMoney pause.

The specific issue that Zoompf was flagging was that Google's `plusone.js` library was being referenced using SSL from a non-SSL page (*http://zoompf.com/blog/2010/03/ zoompf-check-300-or-gateways-got-a-problem*). SSL is important because, if used properly (*https://www.owasp.org/images/4/40/Ivan_Ristic_-Breaking_SSL-_OWASP.pdf*), it provides communications privacy and integrity. However, a CSS file, or JavaScript library, or even a Favicon that is referenced using a SSL-enabled hyperlink from an HTML page which is not served over SSL most likely does not contain information that needs protecting. Since SSL provides these security features with a cost of a decrease in web performance (as discussed later), it is important to only use SSL when you have to.

In this case, the Google `plusone.js` button library does not contain personal or private information. Zoompf's suggestion was to instead retrieve the Google+ library using `http://` instead of `https://`. Here is what Google's documentation has to say (emphasis added):

> The +1 button code requires a script from Google's servers. You may get this error by including the script via `http://` on a page that's loaded via `https://`. We recommend using `https://` to include the script: `<script type="text/javascript" src="https://apis.google.com/js/plusone.js"></script>`. If your web page uses `https://`, some browsers and verification tools will show an error when any assets on the page are called via http://. If your site serves pages via https://, make sure that the +1 button code on those pages also uses https://. (In fact, it's fine to use `https://` in the button code for all pages, even if they are only served via `http://`.)

The "error" that Google is trying to avoid is a mixed content warning. It looks like the one shown in Figure 23-1:

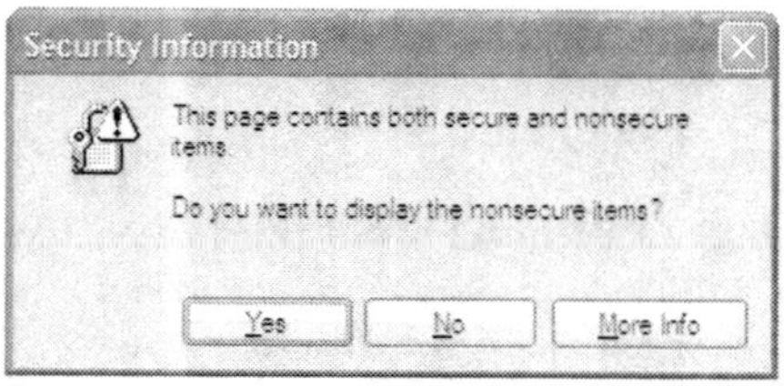

Figure 23-1. Mixed content warning

A mixed content warning happens when an HTML page is served with HTTPS references using HTTP. Due to some serious design flaws (*http://code.google.com/p/browsersec/wiki/Part2*) in modern browsers, mixed content can allow privileged information like the DOM, cookies, referrer URLs, session IDs, and more to be access by untrusted parties. Browsers usually display a confusing dialog box or just fail to render the page, depending on its security settings. Google's solution to avoid all is to just always request the `plusjone.js` file using SSL, even when SSL is not needed.

But using SSL, just for the fun of it, is not a good idea. SSL impacts web performance negatively in several ways:

- HTTPS connections take longer to create than regular HTTP connections (*http://www.semicomplete.com/blog/geekery/ssl-latency.html*). Additional requests may need to be sent to different servers to validate the X.509 certificate chain (*http://www.belshe.com/2011/04/20/certificate-validation-example-facebook/*) before the SSL connection can begin, causing all pending HTTPS connections to that server to block.

- Establishing an HTTPS connection is computationally expensive. The browser and server must do a large amount of work during the SSL handshake (*http://www.bsc .es/media/389.pdf*) and more work encrypting and decrypting data (*http://www.eecs .umich.edu/~taustin/papers/ASPLOS00-crypto.pdf*) as it is sent. While computers are always getting faster SSL overhead is still sufficiently large that an entire market for SSL acceleration (*http://en.wikipedia.org/wiki/SSL_acceleration*) products exists.

- Because HTTPS runs on a separate TCP/IP port than HTTP, your browser cannot use an existing HTTP connection as an HTTPS connection, even if you are talking to the same hostname.

- Using SSL means inline devices like shared caching servers will not see the traffic and cannot be used to improve performance.

- Browser caching of content served over SSL is more complicated than content over HTTP (*http://blogs.msdn.com/b/ieinternals/archive/2010/04/21/internet-explorer -may-bypass-cache-for-cross-domain-https-content.aspx*). Depending on the browser and configuration, content may only be cached in RAM and discarded quickly, or require conditional requests not usually needed.

In short, SSL is great but it's not free. Don't use it if you don't have to.

The solution here is to actually use a protocol-relative URL (*http://blog.httpwatch.com/ 2010/02/10/using-protocol-relative-urls-to-switch-between-http-and-https/*). A protocol-relative URL is a way of referencing a resource on a different host name without specifying what protocol to use to retrieve. So instead of `src="https://apis.goo gle.com/js/plusone.js"` you can use `src="//apis.google.com/js/plusone.js"`. Consider an HTML page which uses a protocol-relative URL to reference `plusone.js`. If the page was served using `https://`, then `plusone.js` is requested using `https://`. Security is maintained and no mixed content security warning will appear. If the page was served using `http://`, then the library will be served using HTTP. No performance hit happens and no caching issues come up either.

Now, I know what you might be thinking: "Did Stoyan seriously allow some guy a spot on the Performance Calendar to talk about protocol relative URLs for eleven paragraphs?" Well yes, I did talk about something cool that many people are not familiar with and that provides an elegant solution to a surprising common problem. (In fact, there tons of other stuff to talk about with protocol relative URLs, like a non-standard IE6 configuration which causes a weird certificate error, or the double downloading bug in IE7 and IE8. So count yourself lucky!) But as I said earlier, the magic of protocol-relative URLs is not the point of this chapter.

The point of chapter is that you need to be careful about performance advice. Not just where you get it, but what it says to do. Google is awesome. They are one of the strongest supporters of web performance in the industry today. But no one is perfect. Mathias improved upon their Google Analytics snippet. Their Google Doodles are always ludicrously high quality JPEGs that needlessly waste bandwidth (*https://twitter.com/*

zoompf/status/144920292446306305). And sometimes, like in this case, their advice is not just right. As the Buddha once said:

> Believe nothing, no matter where you read it, or who has said it, not even if I have said it, unless it agrees with your own reason and your own common sense.

You should always examine a code snippet from a third-party before including it in your site, regardless of who wrote it, even if Steve Souders or Douglas Crockford or John Resig wrote it, to make sure it does not violate any best practices that you already know.

 To comment on this chapter, please visit *http://calendar.perfplanet.com/ 2011/advice-on-trusting-advice/*. Originally published on Dec 23, 2011.

CHAPTER 24

Why You're Probably Reading Your Performance Measurement Results Wrong (At Least You're in Good Company)

Joshua Bixby

One of my favorite books of 2011 was *Thinking, Fast and Slow* (*http://www.amazon .com/Thinking-Fast-Slow-Daniel-Kahneman/dp/0374275637*) by the Nobel Prize-winning psychologist Daniel Kahneman. In his book, Kahneman identifies the two systems of thought that are constantly warring inside our heads:

- System 1, which is fast and intuitive
- System 2, which is slow and logical

Almost invariably, System 1 is flawed, yet we helplessly rely on it. We also have a painful tendency to think we're applying System 2 to our thinking, when in fact it's just an intellectually tarted up version of System 1.

Kahneman offers a nifty little test of this thinking:

> A certain town is served by two hospitals. In the larger hospital about 45 babies are born each day, and in the smaller hospital about 15 babies are born each day. As you know, about 50% of all babies are boys. However the exact percentage varies from day to day. Sometimes it may be higher than 50%, sometimes lower. For a period of 1 year, each hospital recorded the days on which more than 60% of the babies born were boys. Which hospital do you think recorded more such days?

A. The larger hospital
B. The smaller hospital
C. About the same (that is, within 5% of each other)

The correct answer is B, the smaller hospital. But as Kahneman notes, "When this question was posed to a number of undergraduate students, 22% said A; 22% said B; and 56% said C. Sampling theory entails that the expected number of days on which more than 60% of the babies are boys is much greater in the small hospital than in the large hospital, because the large sample is less likely to stray from 50%. This fundamental notion of statistics is evidently not part of people's repertoire of intuition."

But these are just a bunch of cheese-eating undergrads, right? This doesn't apply to our community, because we're all great intuitive statisticians? What was the point of that computer science degree if it didn't allow you a powerful and immediate grasp of stats?

Thinking about Kahneman's findings, I decided to conduct a little test of my own to see how well your average friendly neighborhood web performance expert is able to analyze statistics. (Identities have been hidden to protect the innocent.) Of course, you're allowed to call into question the validity of my test, given its small sample size. I'd be disappointed if you didn't.

The Methodology

I asked 10 very senior and well-respected members of our community to answer the hospital question, above. I also asked them to comment on the results of this little test.

The RUM results shown on Figure 24-1 capture one day of activity on a specific product page for a large e-commerce site for IE9 and Chrome 16. What conclusions would you draw from this table?

Browser Version	Avg. Page Load Time (sec)	Pageviews	Page Load Sample
9.0	4.76	8,142	73
16.0.912.83	3.79	5,605	45

Figure 24-1. RUM results

The Results

If you had to summarize this table, you would probably conclude "Chrome is faster than IE9." That's the story you take away from looking at the table, and you intuitively are drawn to it because that's the part that's interesting to you. The fact the study was done using a specific product page, captures one day of data, or contains 45 timing samples for Chrome is good background information, but isn't relevant to the overall story. Your summary would be the same regardless of the size of the sample, though an absurd sample size (i.e., results captures from two data points or 6 million data points) would probably grab your attention.

Hospital question results: On the hospital question, we were better than the undergrads... but not by much. 5 out of 10 people I surveyed got the question wrong.

RUM results: I was amazed at the lack of focus on the source of the data. Only two people pointed out that the sample size was so low that no meaningful conclusions could be drawn from the results, and that averages were useless for this type of analysis. The other eight all focused on the (assumed) fact that Chrome is faster than IE9, and they told me stories about the improvements in Chrome and how the results are representative of these improvements.

Conclusions

The table and description contain information of two kinds: the story and the source of the story. Our natural tendency is to focus on the story rather than on the reliability of the source, and ultimately we trust our inner statistical gut feel. I am continually amazed at our general failure to appreciate the role of sample size. As a species, we are terrible intuitive statisticians. We are not adequately sensitive to sample size or how we should look at measurement.

Why Does This Matter?

RUM is being adopted in the enterprise at an unprecedented speed. It is becoming our measurement baseline and the ultimate source of truth. For those of us who care about making sites faster in the real world, this is an incredible victory in a long protracted battle against traditional synthetic tests (*http://www.webperformancetoday.com/2011/07/05/web-performance-measurement-island-is-sinking/*).

I now routinely go into enterprises that use RUM. Although I take great satisfaction in winning the war, an important battle now confronts us.

Takeaways

1. We need tools that warn us when our sample sizes are too small. We all learned sampling techniques in high school or university. The risk of error can be calculated for any given sample size by a fairly simple procedure. Don't use your judgement because it is flawed. Not only do we need to be vigilant but we need to lobby for the tool vendors to help us. Google, Gomez, Keynote, and others should notify us when sample sizes are too small—especially given how prone we are to error.

2. Averages are a bad measure for RUM results. RUM results can suffer from significant outliers, which make averages a bad measure in most instances. Unfortunately, averages are used in almost all of the off-the-shelf products I know. If you need to look at one number, look at medians or 95th percentile numbers.

3. Histograms are the best way to graph data. With histograms you can see the distribution of performance measurements and, unlike averages, you can spot outliers that would otherwise skew your results. For example, I took a dataset of 500,000 page

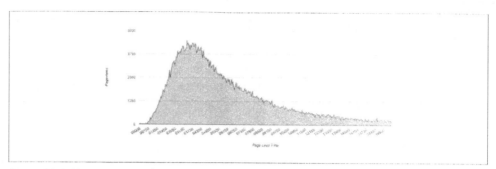

Figure 24-2. Histogram visualization

load time measurements for the same page. If I went with the average load time across all those samples, I'd get a page load time of ~6600msec. Now look at the histogram (Figure 24-2) for all the measurements for the page. Visualizing the measurements in a histogram like this is much much more insightful and tells us a lot more about the performance profile of that page.

(If you're wondering, the median page load time across the data set is ~5350msec. This is probably a more accurate indicator of the page performance and much better than the average, but is not as telling as the histogram that lets us properly visualize the performance profile. As a matter of fact, here at Strangeloop, we usually look at both median and the performance histogram to get the full picture.)

 To comment on this chapter, please visit *http://calendar.perfplanet.com/ 2011/good-company/*. Originally published on Dec 24, 2011.

CHAPTER 25

Lossy Image Compression

Sergey Chernyshev

Images are the one of the oldest items on the Web (right after HTML) and still so little has changed since we started to use them. Yes, we now got JPEG and PNG in addition to original GIF, but other then that, there were not many improvements to make them better.

That is, if you don't count lots of creative talent that went into creating them, so much in fact that it created the Web as we know it now, shiny and full of marketing potential! Without images we wouldn't have the job of building the Web, and without images we wouldn't worry about web performance because there would be no users to care about experience and no business people to pay for improvements.

That being said, images on our websites are the largest payload sent back and forth across the wires of the Net taking a big part in slowing down user experience.

According to HTTPArchive (Figure 25-1, *http://httparchive.org/interesting.php#byte sperpage*), JPEGs, GIFs and PNGs account for *63% of overall page size* and overall image size has 0.64 correlation with overall page load time (Figure 25-2, *http://httparchive.org/ interesting.php#onLoad*).

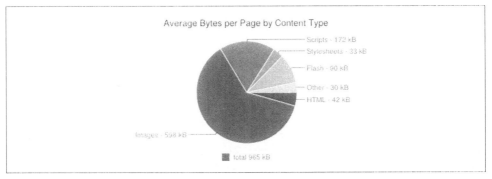

Figure 25-1. Average bytes by content type

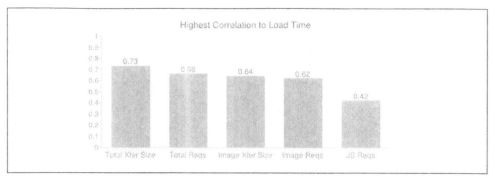

Figure 25-2. Correlation to load times

Still we can safely assume that *we are going to have only more images and they will only grow bigger*, along with the screen resolutions on desktop computers.

Lossy Compression

There are a few different ways to optimize images including compression, spriting, picking appropriate format, resizing and so on. There are many other aspects of handling images that include postloading, caching, URL versioning, CDNs and etc.

In this article I wanted to concentrate on *lossy compression* where *quality characteristics of the images are changed* without significant visual differences for the user, but *with significant changes to performance.*

By now most of us are familiar with loss-less compression, thanks to Stoyan (*http://www.phpied.com/*) and Nicole (*http://www.stubbornella.org/*) who first introduced us to image optimization for web performance with an awesome on-line tool called Smush.it (*http://www.smushit.com/ysmush.it/*) (now run by Yahoo!). There are a few other tools now that have similar functionality for PNG, for example.

With smush.it, image quality is preserved as is with only unnecessary meta-data removed, it often saves up to 30-40% of file size. It is a safe choice and images will be intact when you do that. This seems the only way to go, especially for your design department who believe that once an image comes out of their computers it is sacred and must be preserved absolutely the same.

In reality, quality of the image is not set in stone—JPEG was invented as a format that allowed for size reduction at a price of quality. Web got popular because of images, it wouldn't be here if they were in BMP, TIFF, or PCX formats that were dominating prior to JPEG.

This is why we need to actually start using this feature of JPEG where quality is adjustable. You probably even saw it in settings if you used export functionality of photo editors—Figure 25-3 is a screenshot of quality adjusting section of "export for web and devices" screen in Adobe Photoshop.

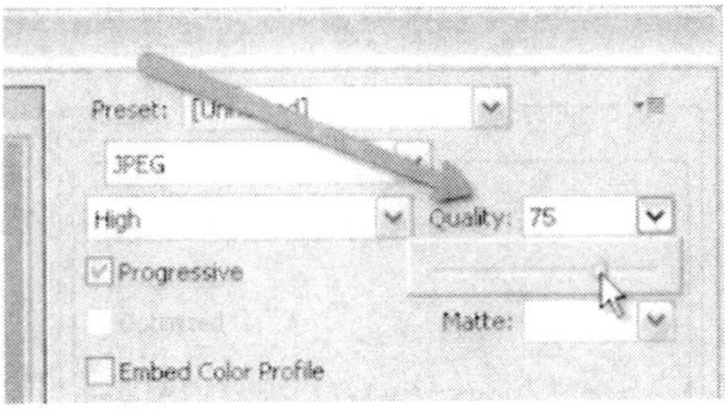

Figure 25-3. JPEG quality settings

Quality setting ranges from 1 to 100 with 75 usually being enough for all photos with some of them looking good enough even with the value of 30. In Photoshop and other tools, you can usually see the differences using your own eyes and adjust appropriately, making sure quality never degrades below certain point, which mainly depends on the image.

Resulting image size heavily depends on the original source of the image and visual features of the picture, sometimes saving up to 80% of the size without significant degradation.

I know these numbers sound pretty vague, but that is exactly the problem that all of us faced when *we needed to automate image optimization*. All images are different and without having a person looking at them, it's *impossible to predict* if fixed quality set tings will damage the images or simply not save them often enough. Unfortunately having a human editor in the middle of the process is costly, time-consuming, and sometimes simply impossible, for example when UGC (user-generated content) is used on the site.

I was bothered by this problem since I saw smush.it doing great job for lossless compression. Luckily, this year, two tools emerged that allow for automation of lossy image compression: one open source tool was developed specifically for WPO purposes by my former co-worker, Ryan Flynn, called ImgMin (*https://github.com/rflynn/imgmin*), and another is a commercial tool called JPEGmini (*http://www.jpegmini.com/*) which came out of consumer photo size reduction.

I can't speak for JPEGmini, their technology (*http://www.jpegmini.com/main/technol ogy*) is private with patents pending, but ImgMin uses a simple approach of trying different quality settings and then picking the result that has the picture difference within a certain threshold. There are a few other simple heuristics, so for more details you can read ImgMin's documentation on Github (*https://github.com/rflynn/imgmin #readme*).

Both of the tools work pretty well, providing different results with ImgMin in its simplicity being less precise. JPEGmini offers dedicated server solution with cloud service coming soon.

In Figure 25-4, you can see my Twitter user pic and how it was *automatically* optimized using loss-less (smush.it) and loss-y (JPEGmini) compression. Notice no perceivable quality degradation between original and optimized images. Results are astonishingly similar on larger photos as well.

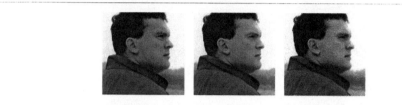

Figure 25-4. Original (10028 bytes), lossless (9834 bytes, 2% savings), lossy (4238 bytes, 58% savings)

This is great news as *it will finally allow us to automate lossy compression*, which was always a manual process—now you can rely on a tool and reliably build it into your image processing pipeline!

To comment on this chapter, please visit *http://calendar.perfplanet.com/2011/lossy-image-compression/*. Originally published on Dec 25, 2011.

CHAPTER 26

Performance Testing with Selenium and JavaScript

JP Castro

Nowadays many websites employ real user monitoring tools such as New Relic (*http://newrelic.com/features/real-user-monitoring*) or Gomez (*http://www.compuware.com/application-performance-management/real-user-monitoring.html*) to measure performance of production applications. Those tools provide a great value by giving real time metrics and allow engineers to identify and address eventual performance bottlenecks.

This works well for live deployed applications, but what about a staged setup? Engineers might want to look at the performance before deploying to production, perhaps while going through a QA process. They may want to find possible performance regressions or make sure a new feature is fast. The staged setup could reside on a corporate network however, restricting the use of RUM tools mentioned earlier.

And what about an application hosted in a firewalled environment? Not all web applications are publicly hosted on the Internet. Some are installed in private data centers for internal use only (think about an intranet type of setup).

How can you watch application performance in these types of scenarios? In this chapter, I'll explain how we leveraged open source software to build our performance test suite.

Recording Data

The initial step is to record data. For that purpose we use a bit of custom code that records time spent on multiple layers: front end, web tier, backend web services, and database.

Our web tier is a traditional server-side MVC application that generates an HTML page for the browser (we use PHP and the Zend Framework, but this could apply to any other technology stack).

First, we store the time at which the server side script started, right before we invoke the MVC framework:

```php
<?php
// store script start time in microseconds
define('START_TIME', microtime(TRUE));
?>
```

Secondly when the MVC framework is ready to buffer the page back to the browser, we insert some inline javascript code which includes:

- The captured start time ("request time")
- The current time ("response time")
- The total time spent doing backend calls (How do we know this information? Our web service client keeps track of the time spent doing webservice calls; and with each webservice response, the backend include the time spent doing database calls).

In addition to those metrics, we include some jquery code to capture:

- The document ready event time
- The window onload event time
- The time of the last click (which we store in a cookie for the next page load)

In other words, in in our HTML document (somewhere toward the end), we have a few lines of javascript that look like this:

```javascript
<script>
Perf = Perf || {};
Perf.requestTime = <?= START_TIME ?>;
Perf.responseTime = <?= microtime(TRUE) ?>;
Perf.wsTime = <?= $wsTime ?>;
Perf.dbTime = <?= $soapTime ?>;
$(document).ready(function(){
  Perf.readyTime = new Date().getTime()/1000;
});
$(window).bind("load", function(){
  Perf.renderTime = new Date().getTime()/1000;
  Perf.clickTime = getLastClickTime();
});
$(window).bind("unload", function(){
  storeLastClickTime(new Date().getTime()/1000);
});
</script>
```

Finally, we insert a couple more javascript lines in the head tag, so that we can record an approximate time at which the page was received by the browser. As Alois Reitbauer pointed out in Timing the Web (*http://calendar.perfplanet.com/2011/timing-the-web/*), this is an approximation as it does not account for things like DNS lookups.

```html
<head>
<script>
```

```
Perf = Perf || {};
Perf.receivedTime = new Date().getTime()/1000;
</script>
[...] more code [...]
</head>
```

Now that we have some metrics for a given request in the browser, how do we retrieve them so that we can examine them?

Collecting and Analyzing the Data

This is where Selenium comes into play. We use Selenium to simulate a person using our web application. Again this is technology agnostic as you can control Selenium from various languages (we use PHP and PHPUnit, but you could do the same with python or ruby).

Selenium has an API that you can call to invoke some javascript snippet and get back the output of the executed code. This API is called getEval.

Within our test code, we first open a page we want to analyze, then use the getEval API to retrieve the metrics we recorded and finish with storing the metrics for later consumption.

```
class ExampleSeleniumTest extends PHPUnit_Extensions_SeleniumTestCase
{
  public function testLoadSomePage()
  {
    // Open our web application
    $this->open('/');
    // Click a link to load the page we want to analyze
    $this->clickAndWait('Some Page')
    // Use getEval API to retrieve the metrics we recorded
    $metrics = $this->getEval('window.Perf');
    // Call our internal method that will store the metrics for later use
    // Note: we include a reference to the page or to what use case we are testing
    $this->saveMetrics('some-page', $metrics);
  }
}
```

We use this pattern for multiple use cases in our application. Also note that while I used the example of a full page load, our framework also supports collecting metrics for AJAX interactions, which we do quite a lot (for instance remotely loading content triggered by a user click).

One of the great things about using Selenium is multiple browser support. We have a set of virtual machines running various versions of Internet Explorer and Firefox. This enables our performance test suite to run across multiple platforms.

The last piece of the puzzle is analyzing the data we collected. For this purpose, we built a small database-driven application that reads the metrics we collected and plots them. We can apply filters such as specific browser vendor or version, specific use case, specific version of our software, etc. We can then look at the complete data over time.

Figure 26-1 shows the logic we use to plot the data we collected.

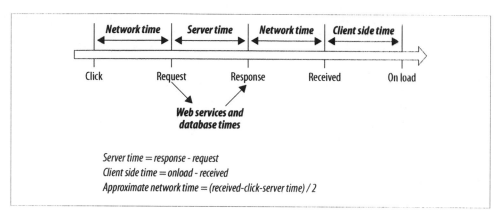

Figure 26-1. Web request times

Sample Results

Figure 26-2 is an example of chart generated after collecting data.

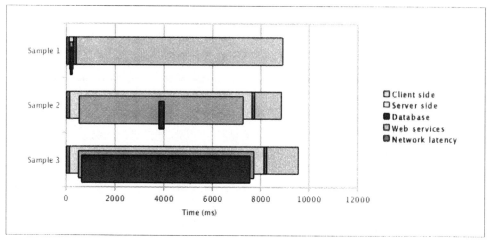

Figure 26-2. Web timings sample

In the above sample, we can observe a client-side performance issue in Sample 1, some inefficient code in the backend web services in Sample 2 and a slow database query in Sample 3.

Benefits

When we built this framework in 2009, we had multiple goals in mind:

- Monitor performance between our software release and catch eventual regressions
- Monitor performance of upcoming features
- Monitor the scalability of the software as we add more users/more data

Looking back, this tool yielded some great results and here are a few examples:

- Discovery of bugs in our javascript code that would result in much higher load times in IE
- Found issues in the way we were manipulating HTML with javascript and were able to improve the responsiveness of the impacted user interactions
- Eliminated bottlenecks in our backend web services as we raised the amount of data: we were able to pinpoint exactly where the problem was (inefficient backend code, slow database queries, etc.)

Closing Words

In conclusion, I'd like to look into some ideas we have in mind to improve our setup.

I'd like to use the tool more often. We currently run the test suite several times during our development process and before each releases, but this is a manual process. It would be great to tie in the test suite with our Jenkins CI builds. A different idea would be to ship the tool as part of our product and run it in production, providing us with some analytics on real world usage of our platform.

As I mentioned, we are using virtual machines to test on multiple platforms. This adds a bit of overhead in terms of maintenance. Maybe we should look at the hosted Selenium solution from Sauce labs (*http://saucelabs.com/ondemand*)?

When we built the product, the performance landscape was a bit different and there are tools today that were not available back then. Would we see any benefits if we were to leverage WebPageTest (*http://code.google.com/p/webpagetest/*), boomerang (*https://github.com/yahoo/boomerang*), etc.?

Credits

I'd like to acknowledge Bill Scott for his presentation on RUM at Netflix (*http://billwscott.com/share/presentations/2008/stanford/HPWP-RealWorld.pdf*), which inspired us to build our framework.

To comment on this chapter, please visit *http://calendar.perfplanet.com/ 2011/performance-testing-with-selenium-and-javascript/*.   Originally published on Dec 26, 2011.

CHAPTER 27

A Simple Way to Measure Website Performance

Pavel Paulau

Not so long ago, folks from Neustar demonstrated at Velocity Conference (*http://veloc ityconf.com/velocity2011/public/schedule/detail/18282*) the possibility of effective client-side performance testing using only free, open-source solutions. They introduced bundle of tools, such as Selenium (*http://code.google.com/p/selenium/*) and Browser-Mob Proxy (*http://opensource.webmetrics.com/browsermob-proxy/*). The first one is intended to automate emulation of user interactions, the second one is a good for metric capturing. That was really inspiring presentation.

The greatest feature of their approach was the fact that all performance data are consolidated into a single container—HTTP Archive (HAR (*http://www.softwareishard .com/blog/har-12-spec/*)). It makes further processing of test results more controlled and predictable due to strict format standardization.

However, there were no advanced tools for dealing with HAR files at that moment. HAR Viewer is wonderful but not suitable for common testing workflow. ShowSlow is instead a perfect example of a repository for automated performance measurement. Unfortunately, handling of HAR files is not the strongest trait of it. So a new project HAR Storage (*http://code.google.com/p/harstorage/*) appeared.

Concept

The testing process is rather straightforward. All you need is to create a Selenium script that describes common user actions. Then you arm your script with methods to control a proxy server via its API. It not only means capturing and storing streams of HTTP requests, but also customization of network characteristics (e.g., bandwidth and latency) and traffic filtering. The last point is extremely important for analysis of the impact of third-party components on overall site performance.

Finally you can send HAR of each page or asynchronous event to local repository—HAR Storage. Actually, HAR Storage (*http://harstorage.com/*) is a simple web application built on Pylons and MongoDB. It allows extracting detailed metrics from HAR files, storing test results, and visualizing all gathered data.

Advantages

The key advantage is high flexibility. With BrowserMob Proxy, you can test a website in any modern browser that supports custom proxy settings. You can even deal with mobile browsers.

Selenium in turn makes it possible to simulate any sophisticated user scenario. Therefore you can analyze both the speed of single page and the performance of complex business transactions.

HAR Storage has cool features too. For instance, you can compare results of different tests. This is a great help for analyzing third-party party content or for investigating the relationship between site speed and network quality (Figure 27-1).

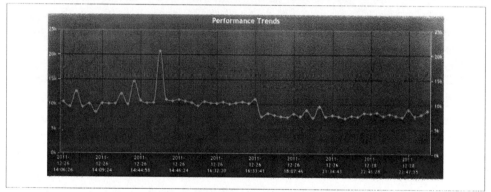

Figure 27-1. Performance Trends

At least with HAR Storage you can continuously track the performance of your website or application at any development phase.

Limitation

Nothing is perfect in this world. BrowserMob proxy runs outside the browser and on the one hand has minimal impact on its performance; on the other hand, internal browser events are inaccessible. Thus you can't estimate performance of rendering or JavaScript parsing. Tools like dynaTrace AJAX Edition (*http://ajax.dynatrace.com/ajax/en/*) are more suitable for such tasks.

This approach may seem too complicated to some people. In fact it isn't. WebPagetest.org (*http://www.webpagetest.org/*) lets you simply put in the URL and enjoy the result. But if you need real cross-browser testing, measurements over time, and implementation of complex use cases—this method will work for you.

Conclusion

Web performance is still critical aspect, and performance testing is still a challenge. Frameworks based on Selenium, BrowserMob Proxy, and HAR Storage may become an ultimate solution for many growing projects.

 To comment on this chapter, please visit *http://calendar.perfplanet.com/ 2011/a-simple-way-to-measure-website-performance/*. Originally published on Dec 27, 2011.

CHAPTER 28

Beyond Bandwidth: UI Performance

David Calhoun

Introduction

Traditionally, older performance studies were concerned with speeding up things on the server side, but a few years back, Steve Souders famously started research on the idea that the main performance bottleneck happened on the client side. In particular, in the way bytes were pushed to the client from the server. "Reduce HTTP requests" has become a general maxim for speeding up frontend performance, and that is a concern that's even more relevant in today's world of mobile browsers (often running on networks that are an order of magnitude slower than broadband connections).

These studies have been concerned with latency and bandwidth, and this still continues to be the focus of performance research today. You are probably already familiar with the standard HTTP waterfall chart (Figure 28-1).

However, we're slowly starting to see a shift to other frontend concerns for each component of the frontend stack (HTML/CSS/JS). In particular, there's a great focus on JavaScript performance, a fact attested to by the popularity of jsPerf (*http://jsperf .com/*) and the rise of JavaScript profilers.

After the Page Loads: The UI Layer

This is all well and good, but we're missing something equally important: the presentation (UI) layer. Although some UI performance tips have been disseminated throughout the community for years, they are often as an aside, with bandwidth and latency concerns much more at the forefront of research. For instance, where CSS is even a concern, the focus is on reducing CSS filesize (*http://www.stevesouders.com/blog/2010/ 07/03/velocity-top-5-mistakes-of-massive-css/*). But what about expensive CSS selectors? Or CSS that may cause the page to lag horribly as the user scrolls?

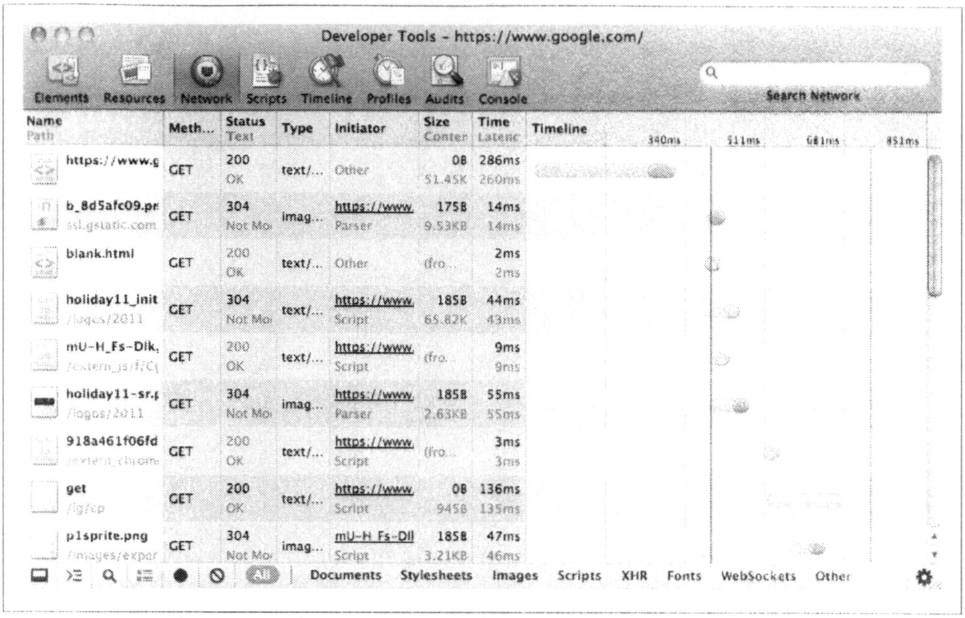

Figure 28-1. HTTP waterfall chart

One of the reasons UI performance has been downplayed is perhaps because of its inability to be quantified. As engineers, it's a bit disconcerting to say that as a result of many hours of improvements, a website "feels" more responsive, or scrolls more smoothly. Without some sort of metrics, it's difficult to determine where the rendering bottlenecks are, or even if we're making progress when trying to smooth them out.

UI Profilers

Luckily we're just now beginning to get access to tools that let us measure these UI bottlenecks. "Reflows" and "repaints" are now more than abstract mysterious happenings—they are now something we can point to on a chart.

At the time of writing, CSS profilers are available in Chrome's Developer Tools, as well as Opera's debugger (Dragonfly). Figure 28-2 shows the new face of performance profiling.

Other than targeting expensive CSS selectors with these new profilers, we also have access to a few more useful tools for UI performance debugging. The following is just a few of these.

CSS Stress Test

CSS Stress Test (*http://andy.edinborough.org/CSS-Stress-Testing-and-Performance-Profiling*) (by Andy Edinborough) is a bookmarklet that figures out which CSS

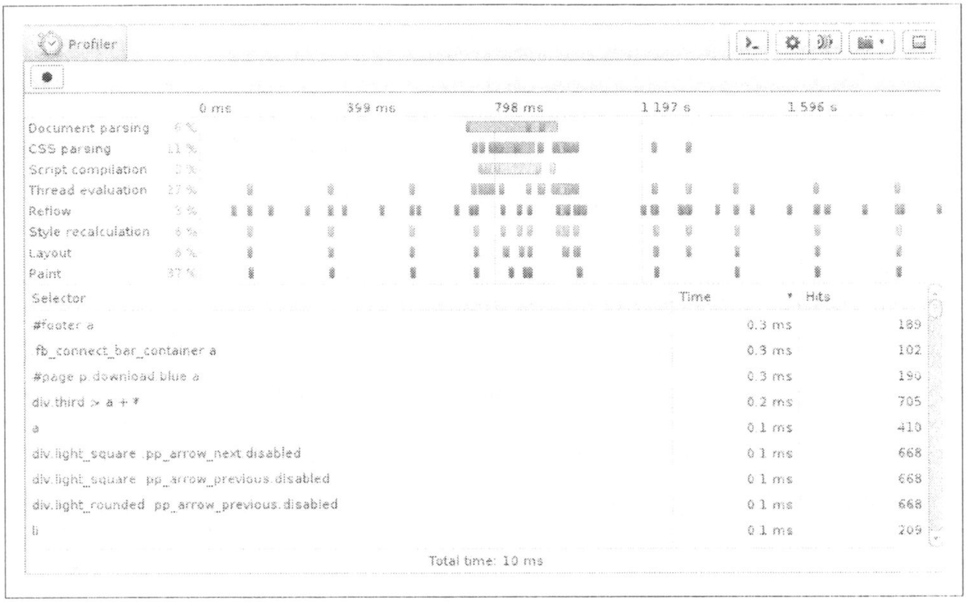

Figure 28-2. Opera profiler

declarations are slowing down the page by selectively removing each one, then subsequently timing the scroll speed performance. The result is a bookmarklet that's a bit jarring to watch, but seems quite useful in tracking down rogue CSS bottlenecks. Note to self: apparently applying border-radius to a ton of elements isn't a very good idea, performance-wise.

CSS Profilers

A CSS profiler (*http://bricss.net/post/13884376788/the-css-profilers-are-coming*) is coming to a browser near you, which will give us much more insight into the actual speed of the CSS we write, moving us forward from vague and mysterious rules. Is the universal selector (*) really that expensive? Are border-radius, box shadow, and rgba values really performance drains? Now we have ways to measure those concerns!

CSS Lint

CSS Lint (*http://csslint.net/*) (by Nicole Sullivan and Nicholas Zakas) is a set of best practices (*https://github.com/stubbornella/csslint/wiki/Rules*) (you may not agree with them all, but that's OK), including a few helpful rules that target UI performance specifically. Run your stylesheets through and it'll give you some helpful tips on what exactly to improve.

DOM Monster

DOM Monster (*http://mir.aculo.us/dom-monster/*) (by Amy Hoy and Thomas Fuchs) is intended as a JavaScript profiler companion, but remember that the complexity of the DOM (Document Object Model) will also affect UI repaints and reflows. Reducing that bloat is better for data down the wire, as well as for both UI rendering and JavaScript DOM access.

Perception of Speed

If you think about it, all of performance is concerned with how performance is perceived by the user. While we're mostly concerned with real performance improvements, we have to recognize the limitations and realize that we don't always have control over bandwidth, latency, or the speed of a user's browser. Where we've already done our best elsewhere, here we sometimes have to fake it. "Fake it 'till you make it!"

What do I mean by faking it? In one circumstance this might mean preloading content where possible, which is what Gmail mobile does before the user clicks on the "Show more messages..." button. After the user clicks, the content has actually already been loaded. It's just a UI sleight-of-hand to show the updated new content, and this happens extremely fast. It doesn't really matter how long it took to make the original HTTP request, because either way the experience is the same for the user, and their *perception* is that the interface is extremely fast. This is just one example of a great marriage of good user experience design with good engineering.

"Faking it" might also mean simply being responsive and quickly showing the user a visual indicator after they take an action. It doesn't matter how well you optimize HTTP requests or how fast the connection is—if you don't give an indication after the user performs an action, they will likely repeat their action (a click or another tap on the touchscreen) and come away with just a bitter memory of a sluggish interface.

Another example of a clever technique here is Flickr, after they moved their architecture over from YUI 2 to YUI 3 (see Ross Harmes talk about it here: *http://www.youtube.com/watch?v=05C0GQPKA4g*). Though the Flickr team took advantage of combining HTTP requests, the delay of the initial load meant that a user might start taking actions before the JavaScript was fully loaded, parsed, and executed. Because Flickr progressively enhances their webpages, this means that without JavaScript available, the user gets taken to fallback pages intended for users with JavaScript disabled. And this is precisely where these quick users ended up, because they had taken actions before JavaScript had a chance to override these URLs intended for fallbacks.

Their solution was to load a mini-library in the page to capture all events on the page and queue them back to be replayed later. Most importantly, this small library also provides a UI (a loading spinner) to give the user feedback after taking actions, even if it means nothing had happened, short of the event being queued up to be replayed later when the JavaScript is ready. Again, we see that sometimes it's just important to fake it 'til you make it!

Tidbits

As I mentioned before, UI performance tips have been circulating for quite a while, but they have been somewhat downplayed compared to latency and bandwidth issues.

Here's a collection of tidbits to give you an idea of some of the concerns that are out there:

- Sprites save HTTP requests, but large sprites hog up memory. (*http://blog.vlad1 .com/2009/06/22/to-sprite-or-not-to-sprite/*)
- Pure CSS3 images? Hmm, maybe later (Chapter 11, by Marcel Duran) discusses how pure CSS3 images are awesome but perhaps impractical, as they trade less bandwidth for decreased rendering speed (it turns out that images render faster).
- Microsoft's FishIE Tank (*http://www.microsoft.com/taiwan/promo/ie9/bow/fish _demo/FishTank_demo.html*) is a nice benchmark to test Canvas rendering speed, measured in frames-per-second. You may even find that tweaking the viewport tag on mobile devices may speed up rendering times (*http://29a.ch/2011/5/27/fast -html5-canvas-on-iphone-mobile-safari-performance*).
- CSS gradients are faster than SVG backgrounds. (*http://lea.verou.me/2011/08/css -gradients-are-much-faster-than-svg/*)
- Older WebKit browsers had scrolling/rendering lag with large box shadows (*https: //bugs.webkit.org/show_bug.cgi?id=22102*). Not all CSS3 stuff is ready for prime time, and sometimes images might be the way to go—better UI performance at the expense of more data down the wire.
- CSS radial gradients may be awesome and save the request of an image, but they might have rendering problems in some browsers, particularly Android (*http://code .google.com/p/android/issues/detail?id=767*). We save bandwidth by not requesting an image, but the user experience suffers.
- Avoid IE CSS filters, as they have a performance hit.
- Use hardware-accelerated CSS animations over JavaScript animations where possible, but be aware of limitations (maximum sizes of 1024x1024px in WebKit). If you do end up needing to animate from JavaScript, try using requestAnimation-Frame (*http://hacks.mozilla.org/2011/08/animating-with-javascript-from-setin terval-to-requestanimationframe/*) as opposed to setTimeout/setInterval.

Call for a Focus on UI Performance

Performance is more than pushing bytes over a fence into a browser! Much of the user's experience happens after a page loads, so we should still be concerned about the performance of a "loaded page" experience. This applies to our JavaScript, but equally as important is our CSS and its impact on scroll speed and overall UI responsiveness.

This might mean that we are sometimes better off performance-wise using images instead of new CSS fanciness that's not yet ready for primetime, and it's up to us to weigh the cost and understand the tradeoff! It also helps us appreciate new CSS features or fancy demos while remaining skeptical of their practical use.

More than anything, if you struggled with a UI performance issue and overcame it, the world could learn from your experience! When you blog about it, you save other folks some time—time that could be spending with their families, which is definitely more important. What we need now is more articles from folks like Marcel (*http://calendar .perfplanet.com/2011/pure-css3-images-hmm-maybe-later/*) and Estelle (*http://calendar .perfplanet.com/2011/mobile-ui-performance-considerations/*) who understand that performance goes beyond simply saving bytes.

 To comment on this chapter, please visit *http://calendar.perfplanet.com/ 2011/beyond-bandwidth-ui-performance/*. Originally published on Dec 28, 2011.

CHAPTER 29

CSS Selector Performance Has Changed! (For the Better)

Nicole Sullivan

Great articles, like Dave Hyatt's "Writing Efficient CSS", helped developers adapt to a rudimentary selector matching landscape. We learned from Steve Souders (and others) that selectors match from right to left, and that certain selectors were particularly arduous to match and should best be avoided. For example, we were told that descendant selectors were slow, especially when the right-most selector matched many elements on the page. All this was fantastic information when we had none, but as it turns out, times have changed. Thanks to some amazing work by Antti Koivisto there are many selectors we don't need to worry about anymore.

Antti Koivisto contributes code to WebKit core and recently spent some time optimizing CSS selector matching. In fact, after finishing his work, he said:

> My view is that authors should not need to worry about optimizing selectors (and from what I see, they generally don't), that should be the job of the engine.

Wow! That sounds fantastic to me. I'd love to be able to use selectors in a way that makes sense for my architecture and let the rendering engine handle selector optimization. So, what did he do? Not just one thing, rather he created multiple levels of optimization—we'll take a look at four optimizations in particular:

- Style sharing
- Rule hashes
- Ancestor filters
- Fast path

Style Sharing

Style sharing allows the browser to figure out that one element in the style tree has the same styles as something it has already figured out. Why do the same calculation twice?

For example:

```
<div>
  <p>foo</p>
  <p>bar</p>
</div>
```

If the browser engine has already calculated the styles for the first paragraph, it doesn't need to do so again for the second paragraph. A simple but clever change that saves the browser a lot of work.

Rule Hashes

By now, we all know that the browser matches styles from right to left, so the rightmost selector is really important. Rule hashes break a stylesheet into groups based on the rightmost selector. For example the following stylesheet would be broken into three groups (Table 29-1).

```
a {}
div p {}
div p.legal {}
#sidebar a {}
#sidebar p {}
```

Table 29-1. Selector groups

a	p	p.legal
a {}	div p {}	div p.legal {}
#sidebar a {}	#sidebar p {}	

When the browser uses rule hashes, it doesn't have to look through every single selector in the entire stylesheet, but through a much smaller group of selectors that actually have a chance of matching. Another simple but very clever change that eliminates unnecessary work for every single HTML element on the page!

Ancestor Filters

The ancestor filters are a bit more complex. They are *Probability filters* which calculate the likelihood that a selector will match. For that reason, the ancestor filter can quickly eliminate rules when the element in question doesn't have required matching ancestors. In this case, it tests for descendant and child selectors and matches based on class, id, and tag. Descendant selectors in particular were previously considered to be quite slow because the rendering engine needed to loop through each ancestor node to test for a match. The bloom filter to the rescue.

A bloom filter is a data structure which lets you test if a particular selector is a member of a set. Sounds a lot like selector matching, right? The bloom filter tests whether a CSS rule is a member of the set of rules that match the element you are currently testing. The cool thing about the bloom filter is that false positives are possible, but false negatives are not. That means that if the bloom filter says a selector doesn't match the current element, the browser can stop looking and move on the the next selector. A huge time saver! On the other hand, if the bloom filter says the current selector matches, the browser can continue with normal matching methods to be 100% certain it is a match. Larger stylesheets will have more false positives, so keeping your stylesheets reasonably lean is a good idea.

The ancestor filter makes matching descendant and child selectors very fast. It can also be used to scope otherwise slow selectors to a minimal subtree so the browser only rarely needs to handle less efficient selectors.

Fast Path

Fast path re-implements more general matching logic using a non-recursive, fully in-lined loop. It is used to match selectors that have any combination of:

- Descendant, child, and sub-selector combinators
- Tag, ID, class, and attribute component selectors

Fast Path improved performance across such a large subset of combinators and selectors. In fact, they saw a 25% improvement overall with a two times improvement for descendant and child selectors. As a plus, this has been implemented for querySelectorAll in addition to style matching.

If so many things have improved, what's still slow?

What Is It Still Slow?

According to Antti, direct and indirect adjacent combinators can still be slow, however, ancestor filters and rule hashes can lower the impact as those selectors will only rarely be matched. He also says that there is still a lot of room for webkit to optimize pseudo classes and elements, but regardless they are much faster than trying to do the same thing with JavaScript and DOM manipulations. In fact, though there is still room for improvement, Antti says:

> Used in moderation pretty much everything will perform just fine from the style matching perspective.

I like the sound of that. The take-away is that if we can *keep stylesheet size sane*, and *be reasonable with our selectors*, we don't need to contort ourselves to match yesterday's browser landscape. Bravo, Antti!

Want to learn more? Check out Paul Irish's presentation on CSS performance (*http:// dl.dropbox.com/u/39519/talks/cssperf/index.html*).

 To comment on this chapter, please visit *http://calendar.perfplanet.com/ 2011/css-selector-performance-has-changed-for-the-better/*. Originally published on Dec 29, 2011.

CHAPTER 30

Losing Your Head with PhantomJS and confess.js

James Pearce

We yearn for powerful and reliable ways to judge the performance and user experience of web applications. But for many years, we've had to rely on a variety of approximate techniques to do so: protocol-level synthesis and measurement, cranky browser automation, fragile event scripting—all accompanied with a hunch that we're still not *quite* capturing the behavior of real users using real browsers.

Enter one of this year's most interesting open source projects: PhantomJS (*http://phantomjs.org/*). Thanks to Ariya Hidayat (*http://ariya.ofilabs.com/*), there's a valuable new tool for every web developer's toolbox, providing a headless, yet fully-featured, WebKit browser that can easily be launched off the command line, and then scripted and manipulated with JavaScript.

I've used PhantomJS to underpin confess.js (*https://github.com/jamesgpearce/confess*), a small library that makes it easy to analyze web pages and apps for various purposes. It currently has two main functions: to provide simple page performance profiles, and to generate app cache manifests. Let's take them for a quick spin.

Performance Summaries

Once installed, the simplest thing to do with confess.js is generate a simple performance profile of a given page. Using the PhantomJS browser, the URL is loaded, its timings taken, and a summary output emitted—all with one single command:

```
$> phantomjs confess.js http://calendar.perfplanet.com/2011/ performance
```

Here, the confess.js script is launched with the PhantomJS binary, directed to go to the PerfPlanet blog page, and then expected to generate something like the following:

```
Elapsed load time:   6199ms
    # of resources:      30
```

```
Fastest resource:     408ms; http://calendar.perfplanet.com/wp-content/themes/wpc/style.css
Slowest resource:    3399ms; http://calendar.perfplanet.com/photos/joshua-70tr.jpg
 Total resources:   69080ms

Smallest resource:    2061b; http://calendar.perfplanet.com/wp-content/themes/wpc/style.css
 Largest resource:    8744b; http://calendar.perfplanet.com/photos/joshua-70tr.jpg
 Total resources:   112661b; (at least)
```

Nothing revolutionary about this simple output—apart from the fact that of course, under the cover, this is coming from a real WebKit browser. We're getting solid script-able access to every request and response that the browser is making and receiving, without having to make any changes to the page under test.

So already you might be able to imagine there's a lot more that can be done with this instrumentation. I had some lighthearted fun getting confess.js (with a verbose flag) to emit waterfall charts of a page and its resources, for example—all in technicolor ASCII-art:

```
 1|-------                                                       |
 2|        -----------                                           |
 3|             ----------                                       |
 4|             ---------------------                            |
 5|             -----------                                      |
 6|             -------                                          |
 7|             -------                                          |
 8|             -------                                          |
 9|             -------                                          |
10|                                  ----------                  |
11|                                  ----------------------      |
12|                                  ----                        |
   ...

 1:    1679ms;      -b; http://cnn.com/
 2:    3115ms;      -b; http://www.cnn.com/
 3:    2716ms;      -b; http://z.cdn.turner.com/...css/hplib-min.css
 4:    5465ms;      -b; http://z.cdn.turner.com/...5/js/hplib-min.js
 5:    2952ms;      -b; http://z.cdn.turner.com/.../globallib-min.js
 6:    1681ms;     21b; http://content.dl-rms.co...r/5721/nodetag.js
 7:    1698ms;      -b; http://icompass.insightexpressai.com/97.js
 8:    1743ms;      -b; http://ad.insightexpress...px?publisherID=97
 9:    1706ms;      -b; http://js.revsci.net/gat...gw.js?csid=A09801
10:    2494ms;   7732b; http://i.cdn.turner.com/...ader/hdr-main.gif
11:    5694ms;  44091b; http://i2.cdn.turner.com...quare-t1-main.jpg
12:    1023ms;    858b; http://i.cdn.turner.com/...earch_hp_text.gif
   ...
```

While this might seem a poor alternative to the rich diagnostics that can be gained from, say, the WebKit Web Inspector tools, it does provide a nice way to get a quick overview of the performance profile—and potential bottlenecks—of a page. And, of course, and more importantly, it can be easily extended, run from the command line, automated, and integrated as you wish.

App Cache Manifest

Similarly, we can also use a headless browser to analyze the application's actual content in order to perform a useful task. Although there's a run-time "Chinese wall" in PhantomJS between the JavaScript of the harness and the JavaScript of the page, it's permable enough to allow us to evaluate script functions against the DOM and have simple results structures returned to confess.js.

Why might we want to analyze a page's DOM in an automated way? Well, take the app cache manifest mechanism, for example: it provides a way to mandate to a browser which resources should be explicitly cached for a given application, but, despite a deceptively simple syntax, it can be frustrating to keep track of all the assets you've used. To maximize the benefits of using app cache, you want to ensure that every resource is considered: whether it's an image, a script, a stylesheet—or even resources further referred to from inside those.

This is the perfect job for a headless browser: once a document is loaded, we can examine it to identify the resources it actually uses. Doing this against the real DOM in a real browser makes it far more likely to identify dependencies required by the app at run-time than would be possible through statically analyzing web markup.

And again, something like this could easily become part of an automated build-and-deploy process. For example:

```
$> phantomjs confess.js http://calendar.perfplanet.com/2011/ appcache
```

...will result in the following manifest being generated:

```
CACHE MANIFEST

# This manifest was created by confess.js, http://github.com/jamesgpearce/confess
#
# Time: Fri Dec 23 2011 13:46:42 GMT-0800 (PST)
# Retrieved URL: http://calendar.perfplanet.com/2011/
# User-agent: Mozilla/5.0 (Macintosh; Intel Mac OS X) AppleWebKit/534.34 (KHTML, like Gecko) PhantomJS,

CACHE:
/photos/aaron-70tr.jpg
/photos/alex-70tr.jpg
/photos/alois-70tr.jpg
[...]

http://calendar.perfplanet.com/wp-content/themes/wpc/globe.png

http://calendar.perfplanet.com/wp-content/themes/wpc/style.css

NETWORK:
*
```

Depending on your app, there might be a lot of output here. But the key parts, as far as the eventual user's browser will be concerned, are the CACHE and NETWORK blocks. The latter is always set to the * wildcard, but the former list of explicit resources is built up automatically from the URL you ran the tool against.

For app cache nirvana, you'd simply need to pipe this output to a file, link to it from the <html> element of your target document, and of course ensure that the file, when deployed, is generated with a content type of text/cache-manifest.

As an aside, the list of dependant resources itself is harvested by confess.js in four ways. First, once the document is loaded in PhantomJS, the DOM is traversed, and URLs sought in src and href attributes on script, img, and link elements. Second, the CSSOM of the document's stylesheets is traversed, and property values of the CSS_URI type are sought. Third, the entire DOM is traversed, and the getComputedStyle method picks up any remaining resources. And last, the tool can be configured to watch for additional network requests—just in case, say, some additional content request has been made by a script in the page that would not have been predicted by the contents of the DOM or CSSOM.

(Naturally, there are many useful ways to configure the manifest generation as whole. You can filter in or out URLs in order to, say, exclude certain file types or resources from remote domains. You can also wait for a certain period after the document loads before performing the extraction, in case you know that a deferred script might be adding in references to other resources. There's information about all this in the docs (*https://github.com/jamesgpearce/confess/blob/master/README.md*).)

Onward and Upward

We've just touched on the two simple examples of what can be done with a headless browser approach in general. The technique provides a powerful way to analyze web applications, and get closer to being able to understand real users' experience and real apps' behavior.

I'd certainly urge you to check out PhantomJS (*http://phantomjs.org/*), try scripting some simple activities, and think about how you can use it to understand and automate website and application behavior. (I'm not even sure I mentioned yet that it has the capability to take screenshots, too.) And of course, feel free to give confess.js (*https://github.com/jamesgpearce/confess*) a try, too—with its humble goal of making it easier to help automate some of those common tasks. I'm always accepting pull requests!

But whatever your tools of choice, do have fun on your performance adventures, push the envelope, make the Web a wonderful place.

 To comment on this chapter, please visit *http://calendar.perfplanet.com/ 2011/losing-your-head-with-phantomjs-and-confess-js/*. Originally published on Dec 30, 2011.

CHAPTER 31

Measure Twice, Cut Once

Tom Hughes-Croucher

There is a famous saying in English, "Measure twice, cut once" which is especially important if you do anything with your hands. Once you've cut a piece of wood with a saw and you find you are 5mm too short, it's pretty hard to fix it. While software is hard to waste in the same way you can waste a raw material like wood, you can certainly waste your time.

A resource like this book is a really great tool for finding ideas to apply to your own work. Many of the authors of this book are lucky in that they spend a significant amount of their time optimizing large sites for companies like Facebook, Yahoo!, and Google (and yours truly, Walmart and others). However most developers have lots of other responsibilities other than just performance.

When you have lots of things on your plate, measuring more than pays its way. While it is easy to grab a technique that someone has laid out for you and apply it (and you should), it is also important to make sure you target the issues that affect your site the most. I was at a conference a few years ago about JavaScript and an extremely prominent, talented, and altogether smart JavaScript expert gave a talk about performance optimization. He gave a number of in-depth tips including unrolling loops and other micro-optimizations.

Here is the thing: when you are the author of a framework used by many thousands of sites every hour you spend optimizing the code pays off on every one of those sites. If you make helper functions to use over and over, your work repays itself many fold through each small usage. However, when you only care about the one site you maintain, unrolling loops probably won't make a significant or obvious a difference to your users. Optimization is all about picking the correct targets.

This is where we come back to measuring again. When you don't have a clear understanding of where your bottlenecks are, you need to measure before you cut. Measuring performance can be done in many ways and this is also important to consider. Unrolling loops in JavaScript is a very atomic micro-optimization. It improves one specific function. However, unrolling a loop that loops only twice and is only used by 1% of users is clearly not an important use of time.

The key to measurement is instrumentation. Start at a macro level. What are the most important parts of your site? These might be the ones used the most, or the ones that have the most impact on your business (such as the checkout process). You might find yourself surprised, perhaps you receive a lot of search engine traffic to a page deep in your site that is poorly optimized. Improving that page by 50% might make a much bigger impact than spending the same time getting another 1% improvement on your already optimized homepage. The only way to really know which pages on your site are important is to look at the stats or to discuss priorities with whoever is in charge of the site.

Once you know what's important, the next task is to figure out what users do with those pages, or again what you want them to do. It's important to note in this process that what customers do now may be an attribute of the current site and not actually what you want them to do. Identify which parts of your site are used the most by finding the most common tasks on the page. Which page level items (menus, search results) do users interact with most?

Here is our formula for optimizing:

- Step 1. Use instrumentation to pick which pages/sections to optimize
- Step 2. Use instrumentation to pick which features to optimize
- Step 3. Optimize

Measure twice, cut once.

Identifying Pages/Sections

How do you go about picking which pages or sections of your site to optimize? This probably one of the easiest tasks because most conventional metrics give you everything you need to know. Start by seeing which pages get the most views. This will give you a short list of obvious targets. Your homepage is almost certainly one them, and then other popular pages on your site. These should be your short list.

The next thing to do is talk to your business owner. That might be your project manager, CEO, whoever. The most popular pages are not always the most important to the business. Checkout and shopping cart are very obvious examples here. If you run an e-commerce site many many people will browse many items, but only a small percentage of people will check out. This doesn't mean check-out isn't important. On the contrary. Checkout is really important, it's just something that metrics may not help you prioritize.

Now you should have a list of the pages or sections of your site that are a mix of the most popular or important ones to the business. This is your hit list. Keep it up-to-date periodically. Until you've exhausted your hit list don't bother with other performance issues.

Identifying Features

On modern websites many pages share the same code on many pages. Looking at the code to find these features or use a packet sniffer like Wireshark (*http://www.wireshark .org/*), Charles Proxy (*http://www.charlesproxy.com/*), or the Chrome Inspector on your hit list pages. This will help you get a list of the external resources (CSS, scripts, images, etc.) that were used by the most pages. You can also examine your HTTP logs to look at what data resources (web services) are being requested for those popular pages. Those resources could also be a blocking factor in page rendering.

You should also try to identify what your users are doing on each page. This can be difficult. Unless you have a very rich metrics system you probably don't know where the users' cursors are, or how much they scroll. What you can probably do, however is look at what where they commonly click to from your history list pages. This will give you an idea of what is being used the most. For example, on an product description page it might be the "Add to Cart" button. You should also look at timing, things like navigation menu items are going to get clicked a lot sooner after rendering than an "Add to Cart" button in general. This is because when people buy things, they normally read the product description first. When they are navigating, they aren't reading page content yet. You can instrument your pages with JavaScript or you can compute the time between page loads per user if you want to be a clever-clogs using a project like Boomerang (*https://github.com/yahoo/boomerang*).

In general the goal is to figure out which things the user will need most readily. As an informal rule of thumb consider prioritizing items to load in this order:

- Items above the fold
- Navigation item (Menus, search bar)
- Items that provide information (Product description, News stories)
- Items to take an action (Add to cart, etc)
- Items below the fold

You can check how fast various things load on your site by using WebPageTest's film strip feature.

Optimizing

The final step is, of course, optimizing. Remember even within optimizing a feature, don't spend all your time optimizing something that is already optimized when there is something used 90% as much that isn't. That's the point of metrics, to make good decisions. This goes both for your list of pages and features, and within the code. The goal of optimizing should be to take your measurements and then make the best use of your time to affect the users' experience. Check out page rendering and JavaScript profilers and techniques. There are lots of resources out there, once you know what you need to optimize, go and find something to solve your problem, and then measure, measure again.

 To comment on this chapter, please visit *http://calendar.perfplanet.com/ 2011/measure-twice-cut-once/*. Originally published on Dec 31, 2011.

CHAPTER 32

When Good Backends Go Bad

Patrick Meenan

There has been a fair amount of research (*http://www.yuiblog.com/blog/2006/11/28/ performance-research-part-1/*) that tells us that 80% to 90% of the time spent loading web pages is spent on the frontend (browser pulling in external resources like CSS, JavaScript, and images) and only 10% to 20% of the time for a typical page is spent on the backend. While that is true in general, and there are a lot of tools that focus on giving you suggestions on improving your frontend code WebPagetest (*http://www .webpagetest.org/*), Page Speed (*http://code.google.com/speed/page-speed/*), Y-Slow (*http://developer.yahoo.com/yslow/*), it is not uncommon to see backend performance issues, particularly as you move away from the top Internet sites into the long tail of the Internet.

This is not entirely unexpected because the top sites tend to have dedicated developers who custom-built the backend code for serving pages, have dedicated operations teams that watch the performance of the systems and databases, and spend a lot of time focused on the performance and scalability of the backends.

As you move out of the top tier of Internet publishers, you start running into sites that are running on off-the-shelf content systems (Drupal, WordPress, Joomla, etc.), and with owners who either contracted for the site development at one point in time or used and tweaked an available template and then used a collection of plug-ins to put together their site (often not knowing how the plug-ins themselves work). The hosting for these sites also varies wildly from dedicated servers to VPS systems to running on shared hosting (by far the most common) where they have little to no insight on the performance of the actual systems their site is running on.

As a result, it's not uncommon to see something like shown on Figure 32-1.

Yes, that is a 30+ second time to first byte (TTFB) with all of the time being spent somewhere on the backend to assemble and produce the page. This wasn't an outlier either. For this page, *every* page load takes 30+ seconds before the browser even gets the first bit of HTML to work on.

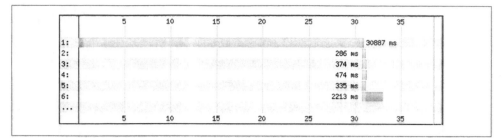

Figure 32-1. 30-second TTFB

This isn't unique to this site or the Content Management System (CMS) it runs on (though it is an extreme example). It is not uncommon to see and 8-to-20 second back-end times from virtually all the different CMS systems (Figure 32-2).

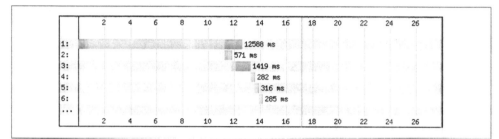

Figure 32-2. 12-second TTFB

This is really painful for users (assuming any of them actually wait that long for the site), but it also causes scaling problems for the backend because the application is tied up for a long time processing each request, making fewer resources available for other users.

What Is a Good Backend Time?

A good target for just the processing time for backend requests is on the order of 100ms (0.1 seconds). That doesn't mean you should expect a TTFB of 100ms, just that the backend processing time shouldn't take longer than that. It is important to remember that the user can't see *anything* at all before the TTFB, so any improvements there go directly to the user experience.

When figuring out the backend time from a frontend tool like WebPagetest, you need to remember to include the network latency. For that, I usually use the socket connect time to the server (orange bar) as the RTT and then use that as a baseline for everything else (Figure 32-3).

In this case, the DNS lookup time (teal bar) is taking longer than I would expect but you want to compare the size of the orange bar to the size of the light green bar. The

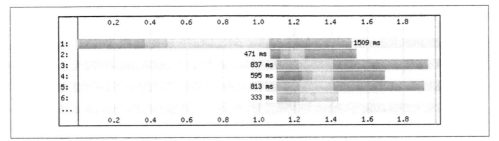

Figure 32-3. 1.5-second TTFB

length of the orange bar is the fastest the server would be able to reply and assumes 0 backend processing time, so if they are reasonably close in size then you're in pretty good shape.

Eyeballing waterfalls is good for a general feeling but if you want to see the specifics, you can get the individual component times in a data table below the waterfalls on WebPagetest (Figure 32-4).

		Request Details		
DNS Lookup	Initial Connection	SSL Negotiation	Time to First Byte	Content Download
368 ms	125 ms		561 ms	455 ms

Figure 32-4. Request timing details

In this case, you just subtract the initial connection time from the TTFB and you have the amount of time that was spent on the backend (436ms here).

Figuring Out What Is Going On

So, you know you have a backend issue, how do you figure out what is causing the problem?

The problem is almost certainly caused by one of these issues:

- Web server configuration that is out of available clients to process requests
- Slow database queries
- Backend calls to external services

Unfortunately, most of the performance tools you are used to using don't have any visibility into those components and they become a black box. At this point, you need a developer and a sysadmin (or someone with the skillset to do both) because fixing it is going to involve code or site configuration changes. Even just finding the source of the problem requires a pretty decent skillset.

There are commercial solutions that will identify the issue for you really quickly with minimal work. Actually, there is a whole sector focused on it (called Application Performance Management or APM). I'll use New Relic (*http://newrelic.com/*) as an example here because it is what I use on webpagetest.org but Dynatrace (*http://www.dynatrace.com/*) is another common solution. All of them require that you install binary code on the server though, so if you are on shared hosting these may not be available options (and once you get through the free trial phase most cost more than shared hosting plans anyway).

Once configured, the APM tools will monitor your production systems and tell you how much time your server is spending in the various different tiers (Figure 32-5).

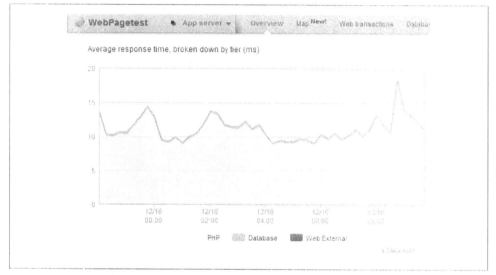

Figure 32-5. New Relic summary

I've done a fair bit of tuning to WebPagetest, so there's not a whole lot to see here. Average response times are ~10ms and the database is only used for the forums so the bulk of the time is spent in the actual application code.

From there you can drill into each band to see exactly where that time is going (Figure 32-6).

In my case, most of the CPU time is spent generating thumbnail images (which includes waterfall thumbnails) for the results pages. Not completely unexpected since they are all generated dynamically by code.

The thumbnail generation is something I spent a fair amount of time optimizing because it used to be a *lot* more resource intensive and took close to 80% of the time. The tools let you keep drilling in to see what specific functions contribute to the time (Figure 32-7).

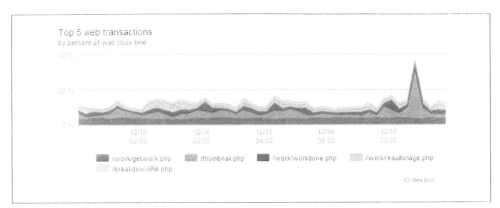

Figure 32-6. New Relic transactions

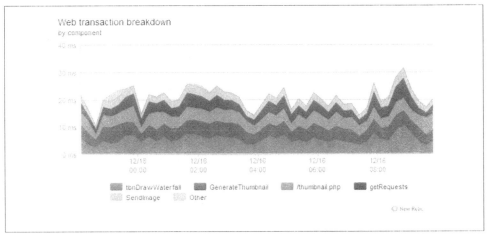

Figure 32-7. New Relic thumbnail details

They let you do the same for database calls, and for particularly slow requests, they will provide diagnostics for individual requests instead of just aggregate results so you can also drill into slow outliers easily.

If you aren't fortunate enough to be able to use the tools, then you have to look into what is available for your platform to see if there are free diagnostic tools or you have to start instrumenting the code yourself. In WordPress, for example, there are several plug-ins that will debug the database queries and tell you how long they are taking.

W3 Total Cache is a useful plug-in for improving WordPress performance but it also provides debugging information that will help you identify any slow database calls (Figure 32-8).

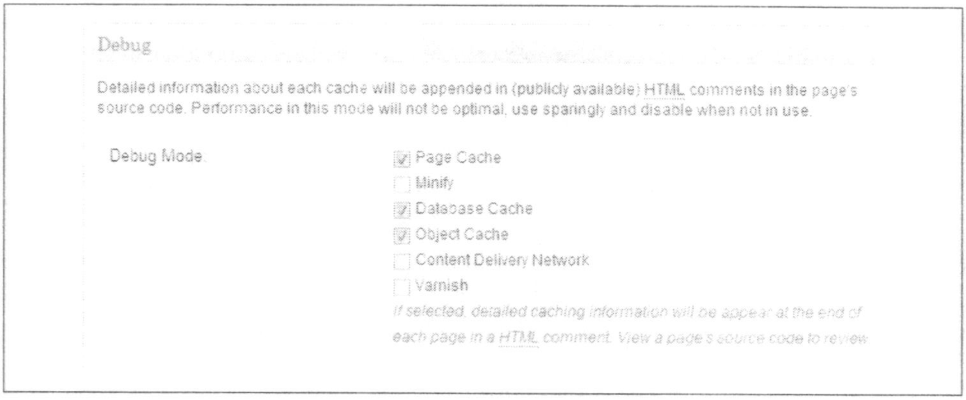

Figure 32-8. W3 Total Cache debug settings

When you enable the debug information, details about every database query (and cache operation) will be logged into the page HTML as a comment that you can view by visiting the page and viewing the page source (Figure 32-9).

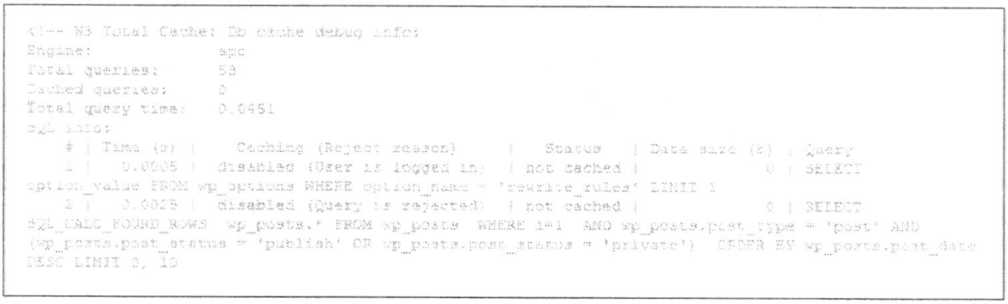

```
<!-- W3 Total Cache: Db cache debug info:
Engine:             apc
Total queries:      53
Cached queries:     0
Total query time:   0.0451
SQL info:
    # | Time (s) |    Caching (Reject reason)     |   Status   | Data size (b) | Query
    1 |   0.0005 |  disabled (User is logged in)  | not cached |             0 | SELECT
option_value FROM wp_options WHERE option_name = 'rewrite_rules' LIMIT 1
    2 |   0.0025 |  disabled (Query is rejected)  | not cached |             0 | SELECT
SQL_CALC_FOUND_ROWS  wp_posts.* FROM wp_posts  WHERE 1=1  AND wp_posts.post_type = 'post' AND
(wp_posts.post_status = 'publish' OR wp_posts.post_status = 'private')  ORDER BY wp_posts.post_date
DESC LIMIT 0, 10
```

Figure 32-9. W3 Total Cache debug data

You'll get the overall time spent in database queries as well as timings and details for each and every query.

Fixing It

Great, so now that you've identified the issues the real hard work starts. The most common "solution" people use is to add caching to hide the problem. This can be in the form of a plug-in like W3 Total Cache that will let you cache all sorts of different operations to custom query caches by using memcache. Caches are absolutely necessary but you should improve the underlying issue as much as possible before enabling caching, that way 100% of the requests will get improved performance.

Finally

As they say in carpentry, measure twice, cut once. Don't go optimizing your site until you have measured the user experience and then use the measurements to guide your work, not grades or scores from various tools—they may not be relevant to your particular situation. Just because sites *normally* spend most of their time on the frontend doesn't mean that is necessarily the case for yours.

 To comment on this chapter, please visit *http://calendar.perfplanet.com/ 2011/when-good-back-ends-go-bad/*. Originally published on Dec 31, 2011.

CHAPTER 33

Web Font Performance: Weighing @font-face Options and Alternatives

Dave Artz

Web fonts are a key ingredient in today's website designs; at my employer (AOL) it is a given that redesigns will feature downloadable fonts. The days of maintaining a sprite full of graphic text headlines are behind us. We've moved on—but what approach yields the best performance?

The goal of this chapter is to look at the various web font implementation options available, benchmark their performance, and arm you with some useful tips in squeezing the most bang for your font byte. I will even throw in a new font loader as a special bonus!

Font Hosting Services Versus Rolling Your Own

There are two approaches you can take to get licensed, downloadable fonts on to your web pages: font hosting services and do-it-yourself (DIY).

Font hosting services
> Typekit, Fonts.com, Fontdeck, etc., provide an easy interface for designers to manage fonts purchased, and generate a link to a dynamic CSS or JavaScript file that serves up the font. Google even provides this service *for free*. Typekit is the only service to provide additional font hinting to ensure fonts occupy the same pixels across browsers.

The DIY approach
> This involves purchasing a font licensed for web use, and (optionally) using a tool like FontSquirrel's generator to optimize its file size. Then, a cross-browser implementation (*http://www.fontspring.com/blog/the-new-bulletproof-font-face-syntax/*) of the standard @font-face CSS is used to enable the font(s). This approach ultimately provides the best performance.

Both approaches make use of the standard @font-face CSS3 declaration, even when injected via JavaScript. JS font loaders like the one used by Google and Typekit (i.e., WebFont loader (*https://developers.google.com/webfonts/docs/webfont_loader*)) provide CSS classes and callbacks to help manage the "FOUT" that may occur, or response timeouts when downloading the font.

What the FOUT?

FOUT, or "Flash of Unstyled Text," was coined by Paul Irish (*http://paulirish.com/2009/fighting-the-font-face-fout/*) and is the brief display of the fallback font before the web font is downloaded and rendered. This can be a jarring user experience, especially if the font style is significantly different.

FOUT of some form exists in all versions of Internet Explorer and Firefox 3.6 and lower. You can check out the video of my demo (*http://www.artzstudio.com/files/font-perfor mance/fout-demo.html*), preferably in full screen mode, at the 1.6 second mark to see it in action. Figure 33-1 shows a screenshot of the video at 1.6s.

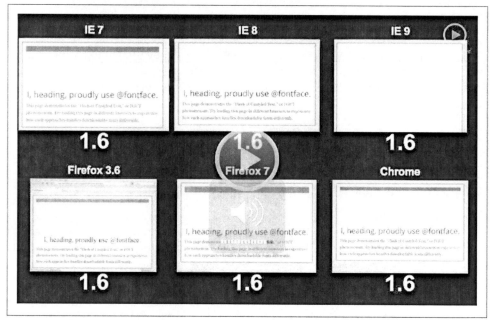

Figure 33-1. FOUT

You'll notice in Internet Explorer 9, the content is blocked until the image has downloaded (http://www.webpagetest.org/video/compare.php?tests=120108_PQ_2SH9D-r:1-c:0). Your guess is as good as mine.

Here are my recommendations for avoiding the FOUT:

- Host the fonts on a CDN (*http://en.wikipedia.org/wiki/Content_delivery_network*).
- GZIP all font files (*http://www.phpied.com/gzip-your-font-face-files/*) except .woff (already compressed).
- Cache all font files for 30+ days by adding a future expires cache header (*http://www.askapache.com/htaccess/apache-speed-cache-control.html*).
- Remove excess glyphs (characters) from the font files.
- Ensure @font-face is the first rule of the first stylesheet on the page (IE).

Still have a FOUT? Read on, a JavaScript font loader may be in order.

Removing Excess Font Glyphs

Font Squirrel has an awesome tool (*http://www.fontsquirrel.com/fontface/generator*) that lets you take a desktop font file and generate its web counterparts. It also allows you to take a subset of the font, significantly reducing file size.

To show just how significant, I added Open Sans and tried all three settings (Figure 33-2).

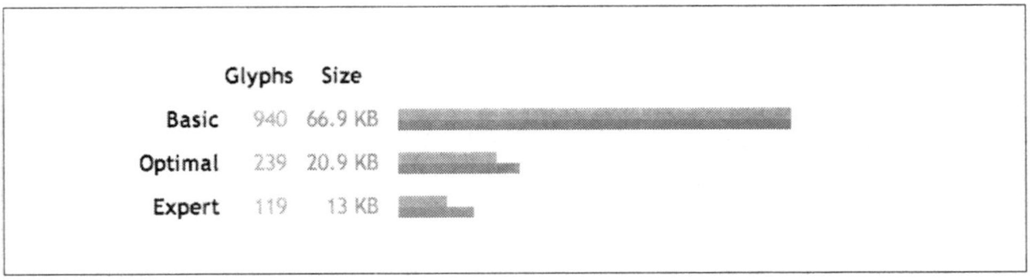

	Glyphs	Size
Basic	940	66.9 KB
Optimal	239	20.9 KB
Expert	119	13 KB

Figure 33-2. Excess glyphs elimination

From the table on Figure 33-2, it should be obvious that the byte size is directly correlated to the number of glyphs (characters) in the font file.

I suggest you follow along with me at Fontsquirrel (http://www.fontsquirrel.com/generator)!

The Basic setting leaves the characters untouched. Optimal reduces the characters to around 256, the Mac Roman character set. We are able to see the greatest savings by selecting Expert mode and only including the *Basic Latin* set, then manually adding in the characters we need.

Here are my recommended Expert FontSquirrel settings (screenshot: *http://www.artzstudio.com/files/font-performance/fontsquirrel-generator-settings.png*):

- Under Rendering, uncheck Fix Vertical Metrics.

- Under Subsetting, check Custom Subsetting.
- Under Unicode Tables, check *only* Basic Latin.

 This assumes the fonts will use only English characters; for other languages, add the characters you need.

- If you are typography nerd, copy and paste ' ' " " into the Single Characters field.
- Verify your Subset Preview; adjust if needed (Figure 33-3).
- Under Advanced Options, give your font a suffix based on the subset (i.e., *latin*).

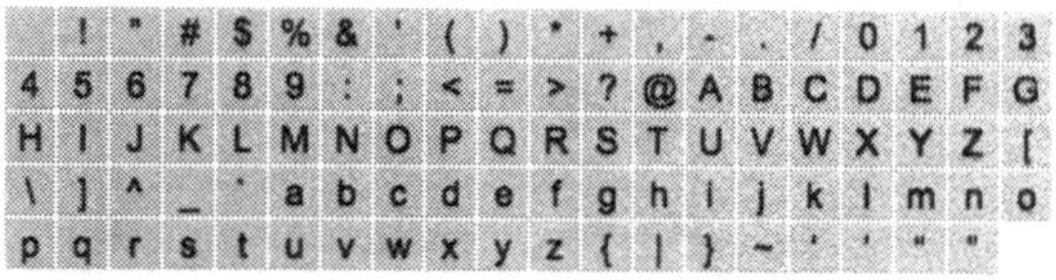

Figure 33-3. Subset preview

JavaScript Font Loaders

Typekit and Google joined forces to create an open source WebFont Loader (*https://developers.google.com/webfonts/docs/webfont_loader*) that provides CSS and JavaScript hooks indicating a font's status as it downloads. This can be useful in normalizing the FOUT across browsers (*http://24ways.org/2010/using-the-webfont-loader-to-make-browsers-behave-the-same*) by hiding the text and adjusting CSS properties so that both fonts occupy the same width.

The three states it tracks are loading, active, and inactive (timeout). Corresponding CSS classes (`wf-loading`, `wf-active`, and `wf-inactive`) can be used to control the FOUT by first hiding headings and then showing them once they're downloaded:

```
h1 {
    visibility: hidden;
}
.wf-active h1 {
    visibility: visible;
}
```

JavaScript hooks for these same events are also available via callbacks in the configuration object:

```
WebFontConfig = {
    google: {
        families: [ 'Tangerine', 'Cantarell' ] // Google example
    },
```

```
    typekit: {
        id: 'myKitId' // Typekit example
    },
    loading: function() {
        // JavaScript to execute when fonts start loading
    },
    active: function() {
        // JavaScript to execute when fonts become active
    },
    inactive: function() {
        // JavaScript to execute when fonts become inactive (time out)
    }
};
```

The WebFont loader also includes callbacks for `fontactive`, `fontloading`, and `fontinactive` that is fired each time a font updates, giving you control at a font level. For more information, check out the WebFont Loader documentation (*https://developers.google.com/webfonts/docs/webfont_loader*).

Introducing Boot.getFont: A Fast and Tiny Web Font Loader

I haven't seen one out there, so I wrote a little font loader that provides the same hooks for loading fonts called `getFont` as part of my Boot library (*https://github.com/artzstudio/Boot*).

It weighs in at 1.4 K after GZIP (versus 6.4 KB Google, 8.3 KB Typekit) and easily fits into your existing library. Simply change the `"Boot"` string at the end of the file to update the namespace (i.e., `jQuery`).

Fonts are loaded via a JavaScript function, and a callback can be supplied that executes after the font has finished rendering.

```
Boot.getFont("opensans", function(){
    // JavaScript to execute when font is active.
});
```

`Boot.getFont` provides similar CSS classes to the WebFont Loader but at a font level, affording precise control:

```
.wf-opensans-loading {
    /* Styles to apply while font is loading. */
}
.wf-opensans-active {
    /* Styles to apply when font is active. */
}
.wf-opensans-inactive {
    /* Styles to apply if font times out. */
}
```

You can easily configure it to grab fonts based on your directory structure by loading a configuration object:

```
// Global
Boot.getFont.option({
```

```
    path: "/fonts/{f}/{f}-webfont" // {f} is replaced with the font name
});

// Font-specific
Boot.getFont({ path: "http://mycdn.com/fonts/{f}/{f}-wf" }, "futura" );
```

I haven't had time to document all the goods, but the library is available here if you are interested.

- Development: boot.getfont.js (*https://raw.github.com/artzstudio/Boot/master/src/ standalone/boot.getfont.js*)

- Production: boot.getfont.min.js (*https://raw.github.com/artzstudio/Boot/master/ src/standalone/boot.getfont.min.js*)

Gentlefonts, Start Your Engines!

Now that you're armed with the knowledge needed to ensure fast-loading fonts, take a look at the performance of the implementation options.

I set up the following test pages, loading the same web font (Open Sans), spanning DIY and various hosting options at Typekit and Google:

- System   (*http://www.artzstudio.com/files/font-performance/benchmark-system .html*): Our control test; this page does not load any fonts and uses Arial.

- FontSquirrel Optimal (*http://www.artzstudio.com/files/font-performance/bench mark-fontsquirrel-optimal.html*): FontSquirrel generator's recommended *Optimal* setting and FontSpring's cross-browser @fontface declaration (*http://www.font spring.com/blog/the-new-bulletproof-font-face-syntax/*). Fonts hosted on the same server as the web page like most small websites.

- FontSquirrel Expert (*http://www.artzstudio.com/files/font-performance/benchmark -fontsquirrel-latin.html*): Used recommended tips above (*http://www.artzstudio .com/2012/02/web-font-performance-weighing-fontface-options-and-alternatives/ #recommended-expert-settings*) to trim font file size using the FontSquirrel Generator, I replaced the *Optimal* font kit in the above test with a minimal *Basic Latin* character set.

- FontSquirrel Expert (CDN) (*http://www.artzstudio.com/files/font-performance/ benchmark-fontsquirrel-latin-cdn.html*): Same as the above test, however fonts are hosted from a CDN on a different domain.

- Boot.getFont   (*http://www.artzstudio.com/files/font-performance/benchmark-get font.html*): This test updated the "FontSquirrel Expert" test to use my `Boot.get Font` JavaScript library.

- Boot.getFont (CDN) (*http://www.artzstudio.com/files/font-performance/bench mark-getfont-cdn.html*): Same as Boot.getFont test, except font files are hosted from a CDN on a different domain.

- Google Web Fonts Standard (*http://www.artzstudio.com/files/font-performance/benchmark-google-standard.html*): I chose Google to represent a free font hosting service, and since this *is* a speed test, and Google is all about speed, I figured they should be in the race. Google provides three implementation options, this being the default—a `<link>` element pointing to a dynamic stylesheet that loads the font(s). *Note: I left out the Import option as results were nearly identical to Standard option.*
- Google Web Fonts JavaScript (*http://www.artzstudio.com/files/font-performance/benchmark-google-import.html*): This option includes the WebFont loader discussed earlier to load the fonts, hosted from Google's servers.
- Typekit (*http://www.artzstudio.com/files/font-performance/benchmark-typekit.html*): Here, I created a kit at Typekit and used the options that provided the smallest font file.

I used *http://webpagetest.org/* and loaded each test page 10 times in Chrome, Firefox 7, IE7, IE8, and IE9 over a 1.5 mbps DSL connection. We are comparing implementation, so I took the fastest test to weed out network latency issues and other causes of variance in the data.

Figure 33-4 shows how they stack up, ranked by the fastest time (ms) across browsers.

Fastest Load Times (ms) by Implementation and Browser

	IE9	IE8	IE7	Firefox	Chrome	Fastest
System	373	358	370	506	398	358
Boot.getFont (CDN)	692	697	696	652	680	652
FontSquirrel Expert (CDN)	710	697	681	667	681	667
Boot.getFont	812	698	798	693	704	693
FontSquirrel Expert	822	704	784	802	792	704
Typekit	798	999	959	795	815	795
FontSquirrel Optimal	997	800	803	933	925	800
Google Web Fonts JavaScript	1096	1097	1126	1254	801	801
Google Web Fonts Standard	896	850	870	1003	899	850

Figure 33-4. Fastest Load Times (ms) by Implementation and Browser

Take some time to digest the data. To better compare implementations across browsers, check out the charts on Figure 33-5 (IE9), Figure 33-6 (IE8), Figure 33-7 (IE7), Figure 33-8 (Firefox), and Figure 33-9 (Chrome).

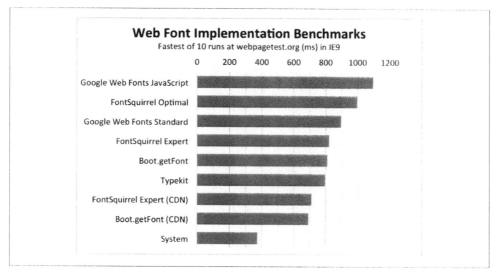

Figure 33-5. Font Implementation Benchmarks: Internet Explorer 9

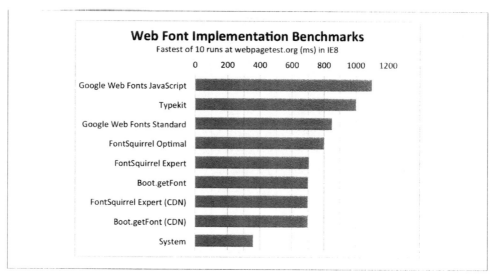

Figure 33-6. Font Implementation Benchmarks: Internet Explorer 8

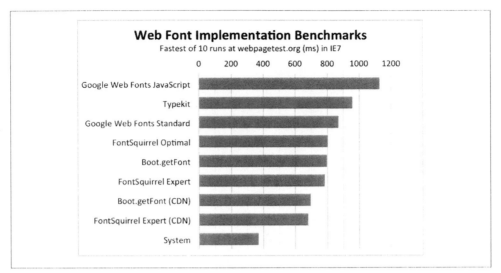

Figure 33-7. Font Implementation Benchmarks: Internet Explorer 7

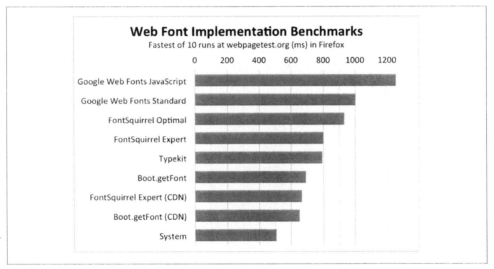

Figure 33-8. Font Implementation Benchmarks: Firefox

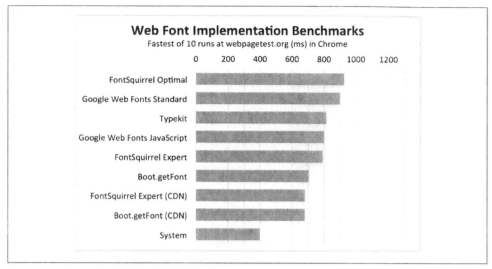

Figure 33-9. Font Implementation Benchmarks: Chrome

My Observations

The Do-It-Yourself implementations were consistently the fastest, especially when combined with a CDN. This is due to physics—less bytes, requests, and CPU overhead are required to serve the font.

It is interesting to compare Google Web Fonts (GWF) to Typekit since they use the same core loader, but that is where the similarities end (Figure 33-10, Figure 33-11).

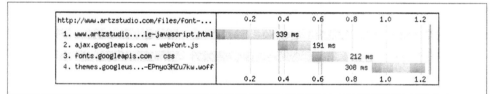

Figure 33-10. Google Web Fonts in Firefox (1254ms): JS→CSS→Font

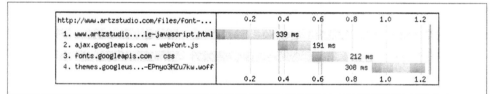

Figure 33-11. Typekit in Firefox (795ms): JS » CSS Data URIs

In browsers that support them, Typekit uses Data URIs in the CSS (*http://www.webpa getest.org/result/111231_2K_2PNEM/10/details/*) to load the font, whereas GWF first loads the JS, then the CSS, and finally the font (*http://www.webpagetest.org/result/111231_13_2PNDW/9/details/*). Typekit uses this approach in IE 8 and lower (*http://www.webpagetest.org/result/111231_QZ_2PNEG/4/details/*) where Data URIs are not supported, ending up with slower load times in those browsers. Google is also slower because of their multiple DNS lookups; Typekit rightly uses one domain for all assets.

I was impressed by the performance of Boot.getFont, which ended up being faster (sometimes by a hair, sometimes more) than the standard @font-face CSS in all cases. My hypothesis is that somehow the JS triggers a reflow/repaint that forces the fonts to download sooner in all browsers.

Final Thoughts

While this article could probably be split into several, I wanted a single place to document implementation choices, tips for optimizing them, and have some reference benchmarks. If other font providers want to hook me up with a free account (and host Open Sans, for consistency), I'd be happy to include them in another study at another time.

I was again disappointed to see Google turn out another (*http://www.artzstudio.com/2011/06/googles-button-is-slow-and-so-is-facebooks/*) slow service. Google friends, take some notes from Typekit!

I am looking forward to hearing your thoughts and observations on this experiment, and to your recommendations for speeding up web fonts. Thanks for reading!

 To comment on this chapter, please visit *http://www.artzstudio.com/2012/02/web-font-performance-weighing-fontface-options-and-alterna tives/*. Originally published on Feb 27, 2012.

Colophon

The animal on the cover of *Web Performance Daybook Volume 2* is a Sugar Squirrel Biak Glider. The squirrel glider (*Petaurus norfolcensis*) is a nocturnal gliding possum, not to be confused with the flying squirrel. The flying squirrel of North America is a placental mammal, while the squirrel glider is a marsupial.

Squirrel gliders are native to the range from the South Australian and Victorian Border through southeast Australia, where they inhabit dry forest and woodlands, to northern Queensland, where they inhabit a wetter eucalypt forest. These wrist-winged gliders make their home in hollowed out trees, lining their dens with leaves. Typically, they live in groups of one male, two females, and offspring.

The squirrel glider's diet consists predominantly of insects and fruit, followed up by tree sap of the Eucalypt and Red Bloodwood variety, pollen, nectar, leaves, and bark. Squirrel gliders have bushy tails comparable to the ring tail possum, and use it as an extra limb to wrap around branches to hold on.

The cover font is Adobe ITC Garamond. The text font is Linotype Birka; the heading font is Adobe Myriad Condensed; and the code font is LucasFont's TheSansMono-Condensed.